WEST POINT

Blue and Gray

WEST POINT

Blue and Gray

Thomas Fleming

ibooks

DISTRIBUTED BY PUBLISHERS GROUP WEST

A Publication of ibooks, inc.

West Point Blue and Gray copyright © 1988, 2005 by Thomas Fleming.
Originally published as *Band of Brothers—West Point in the Civil War*.

Distributed by:
Publishers Group West
1700 Fourth Street, Berkeley, CA 94710
www.pgw.com

ibooks, inc.
24 West 25th Street
New York, NY 10010

ISBN 1-59687-356-6
First ibooks, inc. printing February 2006
10 9 8 7 6 5 4 3 2 1

Printed in the U.S.A.

Contents

1

A School Divided

In the chilly twilight of February 22, 1861, some 250 young men in gray uniforms trudged to the rooms assigned to them as cadets of the United States Military Academy at West Point. Earlier, they had celebrated George Washington's birthday by marching to the chapel to hear one of their professors read Washington's farewell address. They had been ordered to do so by the president of the United States, who wanted them to listen to the "friendly counsel and almost prophetic warnings" in those historic words.

In the small pillared chapel they had gazed up at the familiar painting above the altar. A fierce American eagle was flanked by a pleading woman symbolizing peace and a Roman soldier symbolizing war. The professor read the address, laying particular stress on Washington's advice to "properly estimate the immense value of your national union to your collective and individual happiness."

Now, as they looked out the windows of their rooms at the gray clouds looming above the shrouded humps of the Hudson Highlands, the post band gathered on the far side of the broad tree-lined drill field known as the Plain. With a blare of brass and a rattle of drums, the musicians stepped out.

Across the wintry grass they came to the beat of "Washington's March." With a precision that matched the already famous parading of the cadet corps, the bandsmen closed to a column of fours and swept through the arched sallyport—the entrance to the area between the three-sided cadet barracks. Young men in gray filled every window as the band stamped to a halt. Scarcely missing a beat, they broke into "The Star-Spangled Banner."

At one window, a slim 20-year-old Ohioan named George Armstrong Custer led a cheer for the flag. It resounded across the area from a hundred throats. At an opposite window, Custer's best friend, a swarthy giant from Texas, Thomas Lafayette Rosser, called for a cheer for "Dixie." Back and forth thundered the rival cheers until every throat was hoarse and aching.

The music died away, then the voices. Mournfully, the young men faced each other across the silence. No longer could anyone doubt that West Point—and the United States of America—was fearfully divided.

Founded in 1802, West Point had by this time become, in the opinion of many Americans, "the best school in the world." Those words came from the lips of President Andrew Jackson in the 1830s, but in the intervening years the military academy had maintained the high standards set for it by its first superintendent, Major Sylvanus Thayer. It had won praise from educators such as Horace Mann, who declared he had never seen anything that "equalled the excellence of the teaching or the proficiency of the taught." Foreign visitors were equally extravagant in their praise.

In an era when science was neglected by most American schools, West Point gave its students a first-class education in engineering, mathematics, and physics. Its graduates, after serving an obligatory four years in the army, often resigned to build railroads, bridges, and buildings in a growing United States—and in nations as distant as Russia. No less than forty graduates were professors of mathematics and sixteen taugh civil engineering at civilian colleges. About two-thirds stayed in the country's small regular army of 18,000 men and became professional soldiers. By 1860, about three-quarters of the army's officers were academy graduates.

As military men, West Pointers had proven their value to the nation in the war with Mexico in 1846. They were mostly junior officers, but their staff work and their leadership of companies and battalions enabled the Americans to win stunning victories, even though they were always outnumbered and operating in a foreign country, far from reinforcements and supplies. In two of the American armies, the chief of staff was a West Pointer, although he only had the rank of captain. One commander particularly appreciated their professional skills. On December 10, 1847, at a victory dinner in Mexico City, General Winfield Scott offered a toast to West Point: "But for its science, this army multiplied by four could not have entered the capital of Mexico."

Students came to West Point from all the states in the Union. Each Congressman had the right to appoint one man from his district. The course was difficult and the professor demanding. Approximately a quarter of every class failed to graduate. From the moment a cadet awoke to the reveille bugle at dawn until he crept under his blanket when another bugle blew taps, at 10 P.M., he was under intense scrutiny. He was watched closely by his fellow cadets, his teachers, and the tactical officers who enforced the school's strict discipline and taught him how to drill, use a musket, and handle a cannon.

A cadet was required to recite on every subject that he was studying every day, and he received a mark for his performance. He was also marked for his conduct. If he failed to keep his room scrupulously neat, his shoes shined, and his high-necked gray uniform immaculate, he received demerits. For more serious offenses, such as cooking in his room, he got a heavier bundle of demerits and had to "walk the area" (parade up and down before the barracks with his rifle on his shoulder for hours), do extra guard duty, or be confined to his room. If he received more than 200 demerits in a year, he was expelled.

The atmosphere of the school was intensely military. The students always wore their uniforms—even when playing football, a game that was closer to modern soccer. The cadet corps was organized as a batallion of infantry, with officers and captains from the first (senior) class, sergeants from the second class, and corporals from the third class. Cadet captains were responsible for maintaining discipline in their companies.

In spite of the severity of the course, competition to get into West Point was keen. Some young men spent several years in other colleges before applying, to give them an advantage in the rugged scientific courses. Only about one hundred were admitted in each class. The total enrollment at any given time seldom exceeded three hundred. In this small group, surrounded by military mementos and reminders of patriotism, few cadets could resist the mystique of the corps. Once they were accepted as members, at the end of their plebe (freshman) year, they felt a sense of brotherhood for their fellow cadets that lasted all their lives.

Cadets lived by a lofty moral code, summed up in three words: "Duty, Honor, Country." But the young men of 1861 were the first West Pointers to have to ask themselves if there were deeper meanings behind those noble words. Where did duty lead them, if their home state no longer belonged to their country? What was the honorable thing to do? Was their country the United States of America? Or was it another country, about to be born in Montgomery, Alabama—the Confederate States of America—with a president who was a graduate of West Point?

2

A Country Dividing

On February 8, 1861, Jefferson Davis of West Point's class of 1828 was nominated as president of the Confederate States of America. With great reluctance, he accepted the awesome duty of forming a new nation. In his farewell speech in the United States Senate as senator from Mississippi, Davis made it clear that he left the Union with a heavy heart. But his native state had voted for secession, and he felt he must respond to its summons.

"In the presence of my God," he told the Senate, "I wish you well; and such, I am sure, is the feeling of the people I represent."

No one understood Davis's agony better than his fellow West Pointers. They knew that his emotion rose from the roots of his youth when he had slept in the old stone barracks, drilled on the Plain, and joined the brotherhood of the corps.

Every graduate knew there were two West Points. One was the physical school with its demanding curriculum, its fierce discipline, its fortress-like buildings on the massive outcropping of earth and stone around which the Hudson River flowed. The other school was a spiritual West Point, from which no man ever graduated. He walked with it, or within it, all his life.

Jefferson Davis was walking within it now, deciding in the lonely world of his conscience that the call of his beloved South was a higher duty than his loyalty to the Union. He was hoping that the separation could be made without bloodshed. As a soldier in Mexico, he had distinguished himself at the head of Mississippi's Volunteers. He knew war's bitter harvest of death and suffering. He did not want to see it inflicted on either the South or the North.

Despite desperate efforts to work out a peaceful solution, war soon became inevitable. The nation was about to pay an awful price for the previous decades of sectional hostility. Too many northerners had denounced the Constitution as a "covenant with hell" for condoning Negro slavery and accused southerners of starving and abusing their slaves. Too many southerners had listened to politicians who told them that one soldier from the South could lick ten Yankees and that for every master who mistreated his slaves, there were two white men in the North who abused his factory employees.

West Point had sensed the approaching ordeal of the Union long before the rest of the nation. As early as the 1840s, the cadet corps began dividing into southern and northern companies, although there were many exceptions such as Custer, who spent four years in a southern company. A Massachusetts boy wrote his farmer father in the early 1850s: "Many of the cadets, chiefly those who come from the slavery states, have a great contempt for our Yankee farmers and even pretend to compare them with their slaves."

The Yankee cadet resented this slur. "Whenever any man in conversation with me or in my hearing compares that class [farmers] ... to slaves, I shall always consider it as an insult offered to myself and shall act accordingly."

Southerners, on their side, found it hard to compete in the classroom with the better schooled cadets from New England. One southerner told his sister: "I have no hopes of getting a good standing at this place. There are several Yankees here who know the whole mathematical course ... The Yankees generally take the lead in almost every class."

Southerners consoled themselves by concentrating on the military side of West Point. They claimed to be proud of the way more southerners stayed in the army after graduation, while Yankees tended to resign to take the good jobs being offered to West Pointers by railroads and other industries.

Between North and South stood the westerners, a minority, but growing larger every year, as more and more frontier territories organized themselves into states. Both the quarreling sections admired the easy-going approach of these new-comers to West Point. John Schofield, a future general, told of rooming with "two charming fellows from Virginia" in his plebe year, 1849. "We had hardly learned each other's names when one of them said something [unpleasant] about the Yankees," Schofield recalled.

The Virginian saw anger on Schofield's face and protested: "You are not a Yankee."

"Yes, I am. I'm from Illinois," Schofield said.

"Oh, we don't call western men Yankees."

In that remark Schofield found his mission at West Point: "to be as far as possible a peacemaker between the two hostile sections."

As the decade of the 1850s lengthened, this role became harder and harder to play. North-South brawls exploded on the floor of Congress. A small civil war erupted in Kansas, where northern "Jayhawkers" battled southern "Kickapoo Rangers" to decide whether the state would ban or legalize slavery.

Inevitably the mounting bitterness infiltrated the cadet corps. Fist fights between northern and southern cadets became commonplace. When William Hartz of Pennsylvania, the first captain (the commander of the cadet corps), reported a southern classmate for breaking a regulation, the southerner called Hartz an insulting name. The first captain bloodied his nose and loosened his teeth. The southerner challenged Hartz to a duel. The first captain told him Pennsylvanians considered dueling stupid and silly.

In 1859 came a climactic conflict between two outstanding cadets, Wade Hampton Gibbes of South Carolina and Emory Upton of New York. Ohioan Morris Schaff, who was a plebe that year, called it "the most thrilling event in my life as a cadet." Schaff said it was "really national and prophetic, [the way] this battle between two of her most spirited cadets represented the issue between the states—the courage and bitterness with which it was fought out to the end."

The real cause of the fight was John Brown's raid on Harper's Ferry on October 17, 1859. Brown, a fanatic abolitionist who had fought in Kansas, seized the federal arsenal in that western Virginia town and attempted to launch a slave revolt. His plan fizzled. No slaves rallied to his banner, and federal troops seized Brown and his men after a brief siege.

In their furious discussion of Brown's reckless act, southern cadets singled out Upton as an example of the northern extremism that had inspired Brown. Upton had been a student at Oberlin College in Ohio, an institution which supported abolition and admitted Negro students. During one heated southern gathering, Gibbes remarked that Negro coeds had probably made Upton's stay at Oberlin particularly enjoyable.

A northern cadet overheard the remark and passed it on to Upton. The next day, just after the battalion had broken ranks after marching back from supper, Upton stopped Gibbes and demanded an explanation. Gibbes declined to give one and Upton demanded the right to a "gentleman's satisfaction"—a chance to blacken Gibbes's eyes. Gibbes promptly agreed (he was considerably taller and huskier than Upton) and a room on the first floor of the cadet barracks was selected for the fight.

A wave of excitement swept the corps. "A crowd soon gathered on the pavement, on the stoop and packed into the hall," Morris Schaff recalled. "I gained a place on the stairway. The sentinel, an inexperienced yearling [second year man] was calling loudly for the corporal of the guard, but no one cared for him or his corporal of the guard or any authority vested in them or in anybody else: the excitement was too great. From time to time during the progress of the battle we could hear angry voices, the scuffling of feet and those other dull sounds which fall so heavily on the ear and mean so much."

It was a near-miracle that the fight did not spread to the stairs, where northern and southern cadets were crowded together. One Texas cadet, who was nicknamed "Comanche," howled for his fellow southerners to use bayonets to defend their rights. Finally the door at the head of the stairs opened and Upton stumbled out, his face bleeding. Gibbes had mauled him unmercifully.

John Rogers of Pennsylvania, Upton's roommate, had acted as his second in the fight. He strode to the head of the stairs and looked down on the tangled mob there, while many southerners howled insults at him. With eyes that Schaff described as "glaring like a panther's," he roared: "If there are any more of you down there who want anything, come right up."

No one responded to his challenge. "The South then and there beheld what iron and steel there was in the northern blood when once it was up," Schaff said.

A far more dangerous incident erupted in the middle of a cadet play, later in 1859. One of the scenes called for a saber duel between a cadet from New Jersey and a boy from Virginia. The New Jersey man had stirred southern wrath by making an abolitionist speech while he was home on leave. Both men were good swordsmen and they made the scene come alive with fierce thrusts and deadly lunges until some cadets in the audience could no longer separate illusion from reality.

Suddenly a southerner roared, "Kill him, Jack. Kill him."

Instantly, northern voices shouted: "Go it, Jud."

Fortunately the two swordsmen kept their heads and finished the scene without inflicting any real wounds.

By this time, only the westerners were holding the corps together. Among these, George Armstrong Custer of Ohio was the acknowledged leader. "The rarest man I knew at West Point was Custer," said one cadet, speaking for himself but summing up the opinion of the corps.

Long before he graduated, Custer was a legend. His wildness inspired him to break almost every regulation of the academy. The temptation to talk in ranks, to play forbidden games of cards, to throw snowballs at a passing column, was always more than Custer could resist. Year after year he was within a half dozen demerits of the fatal 200. Somehow he always managed to stop on the brink of expulsion.

Custer was a noted "forager," the cadet term for someone who could get his hands on extra food and smuggle it into his room. A sharp-eyed tactical officer cut short this aspect of his rule-breaking by spotting his stewpot concealed in the chimney of his fireplace. Custer constantly resisted getting his hair cut. After being repeatedly "hived" (given demerits) for long hair, he had himself shaved bald, which further infuriated the tactical officers.

Once, in Spanish class, Custer soberly asked the instructor how to say, "Class dismissed." The instructor pronounced the words, and Custer led his section in a mad bolt out the door.

Most of Custer's friends were southerners. Closest was the big burly Texan, "Tam" Rosser. In letters home, Custer defended his friends. "Southerners have had insult after insult heaped upon them until they are determined no longer to submit to such aggression," he wrote.

The presidential election in November 1860 strained friendships to the breaking point. On the eve of the balloting, a group of southern cadets decided to hold a straw vote at West Point. "A better scheme to embroil the corps and to precipitate hostilities between individuals could not have been devised," wrote Morris Schaff.

The southerners were enraged when the straw vote counters reported sixty-four cadets favored Abraham Lincoln, the Republican candidate. Scarcely a cadet had said a word to anyone about this lanky ex-congressman from Illinois. "It was always a peculiarity, almost childlike in its simplicity, for the Old South to take it for granted that everyone was going its way; it never understood the silence of the puritan," Morris Schaff observed. He had voted for the Democratic candidate, Senator Stephen Douglas of Illinois.

The furious southerners appointed "tellers" to question cadets and find out the names of the "black Republican abolitionists" in the corps. They were disappointed. Not a single cadet admitted he had voted for "the railsplitter," as Lincoln was called. They insisted their vote was a private matter. The questioning sparked violent confrontations between southerners and northerners. Fist fights broke out by the dozen.

Many westerners, such as Custer and Schaff, felt that the southerners were going too far. Their sympathy shifted to the embattled northerners. One day Schaff got into an argument with a southerner over Republican Senator Ben Wade of Ohio.

Although Schaff was a Democrat, he defended his state's senator. The language grew hot and the southerner, who towered over the diminutive Schaff, was about to beat him up when the bugle called everyone to class. On the way back to the barracks after class, Custer and a husky Iowan sidled up to Schaff, who still expected a beating, and said: "If he lays a hand on you, Morris, we'll maul the earth with him."

3
Sad Farewells

In the South after Lincoln's election in 1860, politicians began to discuss secession—the term they used to describe a state's withdrawal from the Union. At West Point on November 19, red-haired Henry S. Farley of South Carolina handed in his resignation—the first member of the cadet corps to withdraw. Four days later, James Hamilton of South Carolina also resigned.

On December 19, another South Carolinian, John T. Wofford, resigned. "There can be no doubt that my native state ... will take her destiny in her own hands for weal or woe," he wrote. "I (being an only son) think it a most sacred duty to protect my mother in time of danger." Friends and family had apparently warned these young men that South Carolina would secede on December 20, 1860.

On December 11, one of Custer's close friends, John "Gimlet" Lea of Mississippi, withdrew. Another Mississippian sent a telegram to the state's governor on December 24: "The war has begun. I leave tomorrow."

The next resignation sent a shock through the corps. Charles P. Ball of Alabama was first sergeant of Company A. That meant he was almost certain to become first captain of the corps, the goal of every ambitious cadet. Morris Schaff described him as "one of those rare young men who carry with them the fascinating mystery of promise." At supper in the mess hall the night that he left, he walked to the door, turned, and called "Attention!" Every man in the battalion rose to his feet. Ball looked at them for a moment, tears in his eyes, then said: "Goodbye, boys. God bless you all." His classmates, in an outburst of pure feeling, hoisted him to their shoulders and carried him down to the wharf, where the steamboat waited.

In the first month of 1861, the Gulf states—Mississippi, Florida, Alabama, Georgia, Louisiana and

Texas—followed South Carolina into secession. But the number of resigning cadets slowed to a trickle. Most of the cadets from these states were struggling with their divided loyalty—and their commitment to West Point. This was especially true of the first classmen. They had spent five long years in study and drill. (An extra year was added to the course in the 1850s in the hope of lowering the number of failures.) Within three heartbreaking months of their goal, these young men hoped against hope that they could graduate.

Many, such as Tam Rosser, and his roommate, a slim handsome Alabamian named John Pelham, were inclined to give up. Pelham, who had won a reputation in the corps for his prowess as a swordsman and boxer, wrote: "It would be exceedingly gratifying to me and I know to the whole family for me to receive a diploma from this institution. But fate seems to have willed it otherwise."

Pelham's father ordered him to wait. Like so many others, he was hoping that the quarrel could be settled short of war.

He was not the only American who persisted in hoping for the best. The new superintendent of West

Point, suave Major Pierre G. T. Beauregard, resented the government's fear that he would resign when his native state, Louisiana, seceded. He insisted he would only resign if secession led to war. "As long as I remain in the service," he told authorities in Washington, "I shall be most scrupulous in the performance of all my obligations to the government." Cadets who came to him for advice got a more down-to-earth response. "Watch me," he told them. "When I jump, you jump. What's the use of jumping too soon?

When Jefferson Davis became president of the Confederacy, there was another flood of resignations from southern cadets. Other southerners continued to cling to a fading hope of peace. John Pelham and Tam Rosser were among them, though they were shaken by a rumor that they might be made prisoners of war after Lincoln's inauguration on March 4. Finally, on February 27, they wrote virtually identical letters to Davis:

> Being still a member of the Mil'y Academy, I don't think it would be exactly proper for me to offer my services to the new government. But I am anxious to serve it to the best of my

ability. If you think it would be better for me to resign now than to wait and graduate, a single word from you will cause me to resign and as soon as my resignation is accepted, I will consider myself under your orders and repair to Montgomery without delay. You know the importance of that portion of the course still to be completed, and also whether my services are needed as present. May I expect a reply if needed?

Events would soon supply an answer to this letter, making a reply from President Davis superfluous. Meanwhile, the young men waited and hoped and wondered. Their divided state of mind is visible in another letter Pelham wrote to his family:

You need not be afraid of piquing my southern feelings by respecting the Stars and Stripes. Although I am a most ultra secessionist, I am still proud of the American flag. It does not belong to the North any more than to us and has never had anything to do with our wrongs. I think both sides ought, in justice to the illustrious dead, lay it aside as a memento of our past greatness and our revolutionary renown. I would fight harder and longer to tear the Stars and Stripes from every northern battlement than for any other cause. They have no right to use it and we should not permit them. It should be stored away with our other household goods, spotless and unstained.

4

War's Whirlwind

In Jefferson Davis's farewell to the United States Senate, he insisted that every state in the nation had always had a right to secede. Abraham Lincoln believed just as firmly in the indivisibility of the Union. In his inaugural address on March 4, 1861, Lincoln appealed to "the better angels of our nature" and urged the seceded states to return to their allegiance.

The plea for peace was ignored by both the North and South. Massachusetts, where abolitionists were numerous, began raising regiments. Early in March, Georgia newspapers published a list of men who might become officers in the state's military forces. All the Georgia cadets at West Point were included.

On March 11, these Georgians had a meeting and Morris Schaff's roommate, John Ashbury West, came back from it to report with deep sadness that he had resigned.

Schaff was heartbroken. West was his closest friend. "Until I knew him well—I made friends slowly—a deep sense of loneliness would come over me at intervals as a cadet, a longing for something," Schaff recalled. "I suppose that something was a friend." Schaff helped West pack his trunk, then walked with him to the "cadet limits"—the point beyond which they could not go without special permission. Neither said a word. They simply threw their arms around each other and turned away, almost sobbing.

Still at the academy were dozens of cadets from the states of the upper South and its borders—North Carolina, Virginia, Arkansas, Tennessee, Kentucky, and Maryland. They watched the mounting tension between Presidents Lincoln and Davis over the ownership of Fort Sumter, at the mouth of Charleston harbor.

For West Pointers, it was a personal drama. The man in command at Sumter was Major Robert

Anderson, who had been at West Point with Jefferson Davis and had fought in Mexico beside him. Born in Kentucky, Anderson was married to a Georgia woman, and he had once owned slaves and a plantation in that state. But duty and honor bound Anderson to defend Fort Sumter until his government ordered him to evacuate it.

Again and again, Anderson refused southern demands to surrender. Opposing him on the Charleston shore was Pierre G. T. Beauregard, who had made the jump from West Point to a general's commission in the Confederacy. Hotheads in the Confederate Congress rammed through a resolution demanding that Davis gain possession of Sumter, "either by negotiation or force." Reluctantly, Davis told Beauregard to send an ultimatum to Major Anderson. He agreed to surrender in two days—when his food was exhausted—if he was not resupplied by the federal government.

There was little chance of a supply ship getting close to Sumter. One had tried it and been driven off by Confederate batteries. But the staff officers who presented Anderson with the ultimatum rejected his request for a two-day delay. They were "ultras," extremists who wanted to settle the quarrel with bullets. Years later, one officer admitted that they feared Presidents Davis and Lincoln might work out a reconciliation and the chance for the war they wanted would have been lost.

At 4:40 A.M. on April 12, 1861, Wade Hampton Gibbes, the cadet who had battered Emory Upton in one of West Point's first outbreaks of North-South violence, pulled the lanyard of a huge mortar and sent the first shell arching high over Charleston harbor to explode above the squat Federal fort with an enormous crash. A moment later, Henry Farley, the first cadet to resign, fired a second shell. The war had begun.

On the morning of April 12, the New York newspapers arrived at West Point, their headlines black with the thunderous news. A wave of excitement swept the nation—and the military academy. All day, as the bombardment continued, the cadets talked of nothing else. For them, as for many other Americans, the southerners were firing on the American flag that flew over Fort Sumter. It stirred depths of patriotism in millions of minds and hearts—and intense feelings at West Point.

That night, Custer, his roommate Tully McCrae, and every other northern and western cadet held a rally in the barracks. "One could have heard us singing 'The Star-Spangled Banner' in Cold Spring," [a town across the Hudson River], McCrae said later. "It was the first time I ever saw the southern contingent cowed. All their northern allies had deserted them and they were stunned."

For the next two days the newspapers continued to describe the shells bursting above the fort, the buildings burning, the smoke surging up over the flagstaff. In a letter to his fiancée on April 13, Tully McCrae wrote:

> I do not know whether I can answer your letter properly or not, for my thoughts are with Major Anderson and his little band who are fighting so bravely against such fearful odds at Fort Sumter ... I suppose this will not interest you, and it is not a proper subject for a letter to a young lady, but I can think of nothing else.

War fever engulfed the academy and the nation when Anderson surrendered the ruins of Sumter after a thirty-four hour bombardment and President Lincoln called for 75,000 volunteers.

In Montgomery, Alabama, the temporary capital of the Confederacy, Jefferson Davis wired General Beauregard that he was glad not one federal soldier had been killed and added: "If occasion offers, tender my friendly remembrance to Major Anderson."

From West Point, Tully McCrae wrote home: "Everything is cast aside. The professors complain bitterly about the deficiency of cadets in their recitations and the superintendent says that something will have to be done about it. I imagine the only way to prevent it is to stop the war."

Fort Sumter inspired "union meetings" in the rooms of dozens of northern and western cadets. Massachusetts and her gathering regiments were cheered. Cadets marched out of the barracks area to the tune of "Yankee Doodle." They ignored regulations and decorated their rooms with paper American flags. A Virginia-born tactical officer ordered Tully McCrae to remove his flags. McCrae responded by painting his water bucket red white and blue. The regulations said nothing about the color of a cadet's bucket.

The day after the firing on Fort Sumter, the Secretary of War ordered all the tactical officers, professors, and cadets at West Point to take a new oath of allegiance. The fifth, or plebe, class was the first group required to take it. Thanks to Tully McCrae, we have a vivid description of the ceremony.

> As it was supposed that some from the slave states would refuse to take the oath, a great many cadets of the other classes had assembled to witness the ceremony. The oath was administered in the chapel in the presence of the military and academic staff in full uniform. Ten of the class refused to take the oath and, of course, will be dismissed. When the first one refused, a few southern cadets tried to applaud him by stamping on the floor. But he was immediately greeted with such a unanimous hiss that he could clearly see the sentiments of the great majority present.

That same day, news of Virginia's secession reached West Point. For almost all the cadets from the upper south and the border states, this meant the bitter parting of the ways. By April 22, thirty-two more cadets had resigned, among them John Pelham and Tam Rosser. For these men the departure was especially heartbreaking because they had passed their final examinations and were within two weeks of graduation. But they decided that they dared not wait any longer if they hoped to reach their native states and play a part in the war.

Unlike Charles Ball of Alabama, who had been carried on the shoulders of his cheering classmates, these young men slipped silently into the night, fearful that a sentry or a policeman might arrest them. Patriotic fervor had reached almost hysterical heights in New York City, and southern sympathizers were in danger of being mobbed. Some cadets took a roundabout route home through Albany, New York, and the Midwest. Others made red, white, and blue rosettes out of ribbons, which they wore in their lapels. Disguised as union patriots, they escaped abuse in New York.

The academy's first class was graduated a month ahead of schedule and received orders to proceed immediately to Washington, D.C. Each cadet was required to take another oath of allegiance to the

United States before receiving his diploma. The corps was overjoyed to learn that not a single cadet refused, though several were from southern states. An emotional scene took place that night in the mess hall when the graduates appeared for supper. Thunderous applause and cheers greeted the new lieutenants. Lower classmen pounded their stools on the floor until they broke to pieces.

A few days later, the cheers had become groans of embarrassment. Five of the forty-five graduates resigned to take commissions in the Confederate army and a sixth followed several weeks later. Most were from the border states, two of which, Tennessee and Arkansas, had not yet seceded when the lieutenants took their oaths and accepted their diplomas.

The shock of these resignations produced a new oath that everyone at West Point was required to take on May 13, 1861. In the old oath cadets simply promised to bear "true faith and allegiance" to the United States of America and obey the orders of the president and officers appointed over them. Now they were required to swear that they would "maintain and defend the sovereignty of the United

States" above "any and all allegiance" they might owe to any state, county, or country.

Two cadets from Kentucky refused to take this oath and were dismissed. Returning home, one boy changed his mind once more, volunteered for the Union army and was later killed in action. Henry A. DuPont of Delaware advised one of his southern friends to take this new oath, arguing that it meant nothing, because the government of the United States had ceased to exist when the southern states seceded. But the boy could not bring himself to kiss the Bible and recite such solemn words. He resigned instead.

The new oath was decisive, as far as determining a cadet's loyalty was concerned. On the day that Lincoln was elected, there were 278 cadets at West Point. Of this number, eighty-six were appointees from southern states. After the final departures on May 13, twenty-one southerners remained at the academy. At other schools, such as Harvard, Yale, Columbia, and Princeton, where, of course, no oath to support the government was required, not a single southern student sided with the North.

Not long after the first class left for Washington, the new first class sent a petition to the Secretary of War asking him to allow them to graduate as soon as possible. The petition received a warm welcome at the War Department. The class departed for Washington on June 24, 1861, with its favorite bad boy, George Armstrong Custer.

Custer, true to his style, was left behind under arrest and threatened with a court martial. A fight had begun in the summer camp while he was officer of the day. Instead of breaking it up, Custer had organized a circle around the combatants and acted as referee. He wound up in the guard-house along with the battling cadets. The superintendent decided to dismiss the charges and let Custer go to war with one more reprimand in his record.

By now, cadets had no illusions about what they were facing. Lieutenant John Grebel, who had been an instructor at West Point in 1858, had been killed in action on June 10, 1861, in a skirmish at Big Bethel, Virginia. The cadets had read the story of his death in the newspapers, as well as accounts of his burial from Independence Hall in Philadelphia. Along with cheers and chances for glory, these young men knew that war meant death for many of them.

On the last Sunday in the chapel every graduating class sang the hymn, "When Shall We Meet Again," which concluded mournfully, "Never, no never." Now the words struck home in a new way. "In all probability," wrote Custer's roommate, Tully McCrae, "in another year the half of them may be in their graves, the victims of war or disease."

5

The Marble Model

The division of mind and heart among West Pointers was not limited to the cadets at the military academy. Lieutenant Colonel Robert E. Lee of West Point's class of 1829 was on duty with his cavalry regiment in Texas when the clash between North and South began. He watched the mounting crisis with horror. "I am not pleased with the course of the cotton states, as they term themselves," he wrote to his son Custis a month after Lincoln's election. "While I wish to do what is right, I am unwilling to do what is wrong either at the bidding of the South or the North. One of their plans seems to be the renewal of the slave trade. That I am opposed to on every ground."

Lee was speaking as a man from Virginia, a state that saw itself as very different from the "cotton states" of the deep south. When Texas seceded, Lee received orders to report to Washington for a meeting with General Winfield Scott, commander of the American Army. As Lee departed, one of his young officers asked him if he intended to "go South or remain North?"

"I shall never bear arms against the Union," Lee answered. "But it may be necessary for me to carry a musket in defense of my native state, Virginia."

Before Lee could leave Texas, his immediate commander, Major General David E. Twiggs, surrendered to the secessionist government. All the regular army officers and men in the state became prisoners of war. Tears welled in Lee's eyes when he heard this news. "Has it come so soon to this?" he asked.

His grief turned to anger a few days later when the Texas rebels told him that if he resigned his commission and joined the Confederacy, he would be treated as a friend. Otherwise, they would not permit him to take his furniture and other possessions out of the state. Lee told them his allegiance was to Virginia and the Union, not to a rebel government in Texas. He went to a friend, asked him to keep an eye on his property, and left for Washington with little but the clothes on his back.

In the capital, Lee received a soldier's ultimate compliment. General Scott, who was too old to lead troops in the field, offered him command of a Union army of 100,000 men with the rank of major general. Lee had been Scott's chief of staff in Mexico and the older man considered him the most brilliant soldier of his generation. After a moment of mournful silence, Lee replied that he could not accept the offer. Although he dreaded the idea of a civil war, he could not in conscience take part in "an invasion of the southern states."

"Lee," Scott said, "you have made the greatest mistake of your life, but I feared it would be so."

Steeped in West Point's creed of duty, honor, country, Lee had hoped that Virginia would stay in the Union. He was dismayed when Scott told him he should resign from the army because his position was "equivocal." The general was telling Lee that a soldier could not have a divided mind about obeying his government.

It took Lee two more days of anguish before he could bring himself to write a letter of resignation. In a note to Scott, he told of "the struggle it has cost me to separate myself from a service to which I have devoted all the best years of my life and all the ability I possessed. Save in defense of my native state, I never desire again to draw my sword."

In his cadet days, Lee had been known as "the marble model." He had been remarkably handsome, with dark curly hair and legs and arms so perfectly proportioned, they seemed to have been carved by a sculptor. He was a good student, graduating second in the class of 1829. In four years he had not received a single demerit for misconduct.

There may have been a touch of envy or sarcasm in the nickname, but there was also considerable admiration. Years later, a fellow classmate wrote that the whole class agreed they had never met a man who better combined a gift for friendship with talents that won respect. "He was full of sympathy and kindness, genial and fond of fun," the classmate recalled. "He was the only one who could laugh at the faults and follies of his friends without touching their affection for him." At the same time, his teasing "confirmed their respect and sense of his superiority."

Lee had distinguished himself as an army engineeer on public works projects such as deepening and protecting the harbor of St. Louis, Missouri. In the Mexican War, he had collected citations for his daring reconnaissances and won even more fame within the army for the way he advised his commander, General Winfield Scott, "with a judgment and tact worthy of all praise."

Lee was also known to younger generations of West Pointers as the school's most popular superintendent. From the day he took command of the military academy in 1852, he had struggled to heal the already mounting quarrel between the North and South. Again and again he had reminded the cadet corps that they were a "band of brothers."

Previous superintendents had insisted on tough discipline. Lee was more like a kindly father than a commanding officer. He worried and fretted over a cadet's problems. If a rule-breaker reformed and started studying, he won praise from the superintendent. If a cadet did not write home, Lee found out why. When he saw a boy was in danger of failing a course, he watched his standing week by week. He would talk over his case with the faculty and discuss it with the cadet himself during the superintendent's daily 7-to-8 A.M. office hour.

Often, Lee urged parents to warn a lazy son to work harder. Sometimes the problem was not laziness but an inability to master higher mathematics, the course that caused most of West Point's failures. In such cases, Lee would ask the parents to let the boy resign rather than go through the humiliation of dismissal. Lee described one of these cadets as "a youth of such fine feelings and good character that I should not like to subject him to the mortification of failure to which he might give more value than it deserves. For I consider the character of no man affected by a want of success provided he has made an honest effort to succeed."

One day when Lee was out riding with his youngest son, Robert, they came upon three cadets who were far beyond the school's limits. Spotting the superintendent, they vaulted over a stone wall and disappeared into the woods. "We rode on for a minute in silence," young Lee recalled. "Then my father said: 'Did you know those young men? But no; if you did, don't say so. I wish boys would do what is right. It would be so much easier on all parties.'"

Lee was always ready to forgive a cadet who repented. Even the few boys who ran away from the military academy and returned days later were given another chance. Once he permitted a cadet who had lied to the officer of the day to remain in the corps when the boy confessed and convinced Lee he had learned a lesson.

Nothing stirred Lee more than a chivalrous gesture. One day, a high-spirited joker from New York, Archibald Gracie, Jr., found a way to torment a fellow cadet, Wharton Green, while parading. Gracie stepped on Green's heels, making him stumble. Gracie did this again and again, and each time the cadet sergeant roared and thundered at Green.

The moment the drill was over, Green proceeded to clobber Gracie. A tactical officer stopped the battle. Green did a vanishing act, but Gracie stood his ground and gave his name and class. The "tac" demanded Green's name and class. "You'll have to ask him; I'm no informer," Gracie replied.

The next morning, Green went to Superintendent Lee during cadet office hours. "Colonel Lee," he said. "Mr. Gracie was yesterday reported for fighting on the parade ground and the other fellow was not."

"Yes, sir," Lee said. "And I presume you are the other fellow?"

"I am, sir, and I wish to submit the case in full for your consideration. Don't you think it very hard on him, Colonel, after getting the worst of the fracas to have to take all the penalty?"

"Admitted," Lee said. "What then?"

"Simply this, sir. Whatever punishment is meted out to him, I insist on having the same given to me."

"The offense entails a heavy penalty," Lee warned.

"I am aware of the fact, Colonel, but Mr. Gracie is not entitled to a monopoly of it."

That was too much gallantry for Lee's Virginian nature to resist. "No, sir," he said. "You will get neither report nor penalty for this and neither will Mr. Gracie. I will cancel the report. Don't you think, Mr. Green, that it is better for brothers to dwell together in peace and harmony?"

"Yes, Colonel," said the young man, "and if we were all like you it would be an easy thing to do."

Lee had a nephew in the cadet corps who did a great deal to promote brotherhood between the North and South—and give the superintendent some gray hairs. Fitzhugh Lee had inherited quantities of his uncle's charm and was enormously popular with his classmates. Part of the reason was his fondness for breaking rules. The wild men like Fitz and Custer were frequently the favorite cadets in their classes.

One night Fitz and two other cadets were caught sneaking back on the post after being absent from the barracks all night. Thanks to this and other escapades, Fitz had piled up 197 demerits by the end of the school year. Three more and he would have been dismissed. Colonel Lee decided to deprive him of his summer leave as a lesser punishment.

One night toward the end of July, Fitz was caught again trying to get back to his tent after another late night ramble. That put him over the 200 mark in demerits and made him a lost cause. Lee could only forward his papers to Washington, D.C., and recommend dismissal.

To the superintendent's surprise (and secret delight), the entire class came to Fitz's rescue. They made a unanimous pledge not to go out of bounds for the rest of the year if Fitz was forgiven. Lee solemnly observed that "from a military point of view" such an agreement between the school and the cadet corps was irregular. But he recommended to the secretary of war that "the pledge be accepted, the charges withdrawn." The secretary agreed and Fitz survived to graduate a lowly forty-fifth in a class of forty-nine in 1856.

Fitz returned to the academy in 1860 for duty as a tactical officer. When Virginia seceded, he decided that his duty was with his state, although he said he did not believe in secession and "hated to desert the old flag." In a letter home, one cadet told how on the night before he left, Fitz "went to every room and shook hands with every one of us and with tears in his eyes said he hoped our recollections of him would be as happy as those that he had of us."

Later that night, Fitz's fellow officers gathered beneath his window and serenaded him, further proof, the letter writer said, that "he was the most popular officer that I have ever seen at West Point."

The next day, as Fitz departed in a horse-drawn omnibus, the cadets gathered in front of the barracks and saluted him by silently doffing their caps—which was the way officers greeted each other in the army at the time. It was the corps' way of saying that it regarded Fitz as a true friend.

Fitz was not Superintendent Lee's favorite cadet, however. That title belonged to a young Virginian named James Ewell Brown Stuart. "Jeb" never let his receding chin trouble him. He always had the best-looking girls on the post swarming around him. His fellow cadets called him "Beauty," in ironic tribute to his ability to overcome his looks.

Once, while serving as orderly sergent in the mess hall, someone made a nasty remark about southerners. Stuart slugged him and soon was the center of a battle involving at least four other cadets. Lee could have punished Jeb severely. But he let him off with a simple reprimand, which he turned into a lecture to the corps about "the evil tendency" of losing one's temper.

Less than a month later, Stuart was in trouble again, this time for talking back to one of his instructors. Again, he had responded instinctively to a slur against the South and again the superintendent could not manage to do more than issue another reprimand. Lee said it was hard to understand why someone of Cadet Stuart's intelligence had failed to see the "impropriety" of his conduct. It was even harder for the superintendent to believe that he "intentionally committed a fault so utterly at variance with his generally correct deportment."

Why did Lee forgive Stuart so easily? One reason was Stuart's wholehearted commitment to the brotherhood of the corps. When an earnest young cadet from Maine, Oliver O. Howard, announced he was an abolitionist, southerners began to "cut" him. They refused to speak to him, or even to notice him. The practice soon spread until it included almost the entire corps. "For a time," Howard said later, "my life at West Point was wretched."

When Howard finally challenged his tormentors and distributed a few black eyes, Jeb Stuart was the first to step forward and shake his hand. "I can never forget his manliness," Howard said. "He spoke to me, he visited me and we became warm friends." Jeb even introduced the solemn young Yankee to his girl friends and this, some say, did more to relax Howard's stiff manner than anything else.

At this time, Jefferson Davis was secretary of war in the cabinet of President Franklin Pierce. He visited West Point and was "surprised to see so many grey hairs" on Lieutenant Colonel Lee's head. Lee confessed that the cadets worried him "exceedingly". He wondered if sympathy with young people might be an "impediment" to his success as a superintendent. A few months later the secretary of war transferred Lee to command of the 2nd Cavalry in Texas, and he left West Point for long years of service on the frontier.

Three days after Lee turned down General Winfield Scott's order and resigned from the army, Virginia asked him to take command of her troops. He soon saw the hopelessness of his desire to sheathe his sword forever. Unlike the demagogues who were boasting that one southern soldier was worth ten Yankees, Lee had no illusions about the desperate nature of the coming conflict. He knew that the South faced terrible disadvantages in manpower and equipment.

Lee made only one recorded comment on Virginia's fateful decision to join the other southern states. While he was paying a druggist's bill in Alexandria, he remarked, "I must say that I am one of these dull creatures that cannot see the good of secession."

6

The Quiet Man

I n Galena, Illinois, another West Pointer was clerking in his family's leather goods store. A small, bearded ex-captain who had resigned from the army, he had less trouble making up his mind where his loyalty lay. When a friend burst into the store to shout the news that the South was seceding and had chosen Jefferson Davis as president, Ulysses S. Grant growled: "Davis and the whole gang of them ought to be hung."

In 1861, few people outside the small circle of West Point graduates had heard of Grant. But Richard S. Ewell, who was to become a Confederate general, remarked in May of 1861, "There is one West Pointer, I think in Missouri, little known and whom I hope the northern people will not find out. I mean Sam Grant. I knew him well at the Academy and in Mexico. I should fear him more than any of their officers I have yet heard of. He is not a man of genius but he is clear-headed, quick and daring."

"Sam" Grant was christened Hiram Ulysses Grant by his parents. He got his nickname when a careless clerk made an error and listed him as Ulysses S. Grant when he entered West Point. On the register of cadets it was shortened to U.S. Grant. Older cadets spotted the initials and whooped, "U.S. Grant, United States Grant. Uncle Sam Grant—Uncle Sam!"

The upperclassmen decided the joke was even funnier when they saw the owner of the name. Uncle Sam Grant was a round-faced boy, only 5 feet one inches tall, and weighing just 117 pounds—the total opposite of the tall, lantern-jawed Uncle Sam, who was the cartoonists' symbol for shrewd, aggressive America. "A more unpromising boy never entered the military academy," declared first classman William Tecumseh Sherman.

Son of a loving mother who had never scolded him, Ulysses Grant found West Point an appalling place. He had no talent for the spit-and-polish soldiering demanded of him. He was sloppy in dress and habits, having spent most of his Ohio life on a horse's back. His feet found it impossible to follow the drum beat of drill and stay in step. His life was one continuous barrage of belittlement.

"Keep step, Mister Grant! You're a hell of an Uncle Sam! Pull that belly in, Mr. Grant! Does your mother know you're out? Who in God's name sent that thing here?" So one biographer describes what Grant heard day after day.

But there was another side to Uncle Sam Grant, which his fellow plebes saw one day and never forgot. A hulking cadet named Jack Lindsay shoved Grant out of his place in line at squad drill. The son of a colonel, Jack had numerous friends on the academy staff, and he thought this gave him the right to be a bully and a loudmouth.

Grant quietly told Lindsay not to shove him again. Lindsay sneered and repeated the performance. Grant flattened him with one punch. His classmates stopped laughing at "Uncle Sam" and shortened the nickname to a good-natured "Sam" which Grant bore without complaint for the rest of his life.

Still, Sam Grant was never able to accept West Point's strict discipline. His attitude is visible in a letter to a cousin:

> I came near to forgetting to tell you about our demerits or black marks. They give a man one of these for almost nothing and if he gets 200 in a year they dismiss him. To show you how easy it is to get one of these, a man by the name of Grant, of this state, got eight for not going to church. He was also put under arrest so he cannot leave his room perhaps for a month; all this for not going to church.

Although Grant collected demerits by the bushel, he had no trouble with West Point's science and mathematics courses. One of his roommates said years later that he was "lazy and careless" in his studies, but he was "so quick in his perceptions that he usually made very fair recitations. In scientific subjects he was very bright, and if he had labored hard he would have stood very high in them."

Sam Grant declined to labor hard. Desperately homesick, he sat in his room reading debates in Congress about a bill to abolish the military academy. "I saw in this an honorable way to obtain a discharge," he later said. The bill got nowhere and Sam Grant drifted through the first year to find himself number twenty-seven among a class of 60. He might have continued to drift downward, perhaps into failure. But something new in the curriculum changed Grant's attitude. From now on, the super-intendent announced, horseback riding and cavalry tactics were to be part of the cadets' military train-ing.

Grant's heart leaped. Above all things, riding was his supreme pleasure, his best skill. As a toddler in his father's tannery, he had wandered between the hoofs of waiting horses, swung from their tails. No matter what he did, his mother remarked, "horses seemed to understand him."

By this time, Grant had acquired some interesting friends. James "Pete" Longstreet of South Carolina was tall, athletic, and intensely military. Lumbering, bearlike Simon Bolivar Buckner of Kentucky looked as if he could fight a war single-handedly. Why these big aggressive men were attracted to stumpy, sloppy Sam Grant would have mystified any out-sider—until he or she saw Grant on horseback.

In later years, Longstreet called him "the most daring horseman in the Academy." Cadets flocked to the riding hall to watch him. "It was as good as a circus to see Grant ride," one recalled. "There was a dark bay horse that was so fractious it was about to be condemned. Grant selected it for his horse. He bridled, mounted and rode it every day at parade; and how he did ride! The whole class would stand around admiring his wonderful command of the beast and his graceful evolution.

Another thing his friends remembered was Grant's unshakeable poise. Blackboard recitations could make the coolest cadets turn pale and sweat, but these ordeals never bothered Sam Grant. One day, a joker added some additional stress to the routine. A cadet brought a big heirloom watch into the engineering class. It was being passed around when the professor arrived. Sam Grant found himself with the watch in his hand. He stuffed it under his coat and quickly buttoned it.

Grant and three other cadets were sent to the board to work out problems. Grant finished his figuring, put down his chalk, and began to explain what he had done. Suddenly—bong, bong, bong,—the antique watch under his coat began striking the hour. One cadet later said it sounded like a Chinese gong.

The professor thought the noise was coming from the hall, but when the door was closed the bongs only got louder. Furious, the professor began hunting under desks and in closets. While the rest of the class practically strangled trying not to laugh, Grant calmly continued his recitation. Eventually he out-talked the alarm and sat down. The professor never figured out where the bongs came from. The corps never forgot Sam Grant's iron nerves.

Grant's coolness also came in handy when he began rooming with a straight-faced Connecticut Yankee named George "Dragon" Deshon. He was one of the top students in the class—and he seldom got a demerit. Only Grant and a few close friends knew that the Dragon was a fearless forager, famed for his ability to steal food for midnight feasts. A complete daredevil behind his mask of obedience, Deshon stole chickens and vegetables not from nearby farmers but from the superintendent himself.

One night, Sam and the Dragon were roasting one of the superintendent's turkeys in their fireplace when the door opened and the tactical officer of the day walked into the room. The two cadets leaped to attention, elbow to elbow in front of the fireplace. The officer, a lieutenant who had just returned from fighting Indians on the frontier, realized what was going on. He could not have failed to notice the smell of roasting turkey filling the room. But he had not yet readjusted to West Point's discipline. He did not see much wrong with cadets doing a little cooking on the side. Frowning ferociously, he stalked around the room, while Grant and Deshon nervously shifted position to keep between him and the turkey. He finally departed after inspecting every inch of the room except the fireplace.

In his studies, Grant remained in the middle of the class of 1843, finishing twenty-first among thirty-nine survivors. He collected 290 demerits in his four years, making him a middle man in conduct, too. But his horsemanship made him the most memorable figure on graduation day. Part of the first class's exercises was a drill in the riding hall. Visitors, professors, and lower classmen crowded the stands as the young horsemen wheeled, brandishing long cavalry sabers. One by one they leaped the bars, finally forming a line in the middle of the long bark-covered floor. The riding master strode to the jumping bar, lifted it higher than his head and called: "Cadet Grant."

Among the spectators, cadets whispered, "He's on York." This was the huge horse Grant had tamed the year before. To the far end of the riding hall went the slim horseman, looking almost ridiculously tiny on the big animal. Down the hall thundered horse and rider, faster and faster—then soaring from the ground "as if man and beast had been welded together" one cadet later said. Grant and York set an academy jump record that stood for twenty-five years.

After graduation, Sam Grant distinguished himself as an infantry officer in the Mexican War. Then his army career dwindled into disgrace and despair. Ordered to isolated army posts in the Far West, he could not afford to bring his wife and children with him. In his loneliness, he began to drink. He lost money that he invested in several businesses and drank even more heavily. Finally, his commanding officer advised him to resign or face court martial charges.

Grant arrived in New York from California with barely a cent in his pocket. He had to borrow money from his old friend Simon Bolivar Buckner to get home to Ohio. His attempts at farming and business were unsuccessful, and he was soon reduced to clerking in his father's leather goods store.

But there was a fierce pride in Grant. In spite of his misfortunes, he remained convinced he was destined for great things. The conviction may have had its roots in a psychic experience he had had during his plebe year at West Point. General Winfield Scott was inspecting the cadet corps. Watching Scott, resplendent in his dress uniform, stalking down the ranks, Sam Grant suddenly *knew* he would do the same thing some day. He would be the army's commander-in-chief.

In spite of this sense of destiny, Grant's second beginning as a soldier was almost as dismal as his first. He wrote a letter to Washington, D.C., offering his services to suppress the southern rebellion. The War Department did not even bother to answer it. Friends finally persuaded the governor of Illinois to appoint him colonel of a volunteer regiment. Grant arrived in the regiment's camp dressed in an old coat, worn out at the elbow, and a battered plug hat. His soldiers were ragged and barefooted, but they had formed a high estimate of what a colonel ought to be. They began making fun of Grant.

"What a colonel! Damn such a colonel!"

A few of them, to show off to the others, got behind Grant's back and began pretending to box with him. While one soldier was doing this, another man pushed him into Grant, knocking off his hat. Without a word, Grant picked up the hat, dusted it off, and put it back on his head. Then he turned and stared at the men who were trying to make fun of him. For the first time the regiment realized the colonel was a soldier.

Walking around the camp, Grant noticed that there was a guard of eighty men with clubs to keep the soldiers from climbing the fence and going into a nearby city in pursuit of women. Grant calmly disbanded the guard and told the gaping recruits that from now on each man must be present at roll call: there would be several each day.

"The effect of that order was wonderful," recalled one of the regiment's junior officers. "There was no more climbing the fence after that."

The regiment found it hard to understand their new colonel. "He was soon called the 'Quiet Man,'" one of the privates said. "In a few days he reduced matters in camp to perfect order."

7

The Sum of All Evils

In Virginia, the students and faculty of another school for soldiers, the Virginia Military Institute, also prepared for war. One of the faculty members was Thomas. J. Jackson, professor of artillery tactics and natural philosophy. An 1846 graduate of West Point, Jackson was, like Sam Grant, totally unknown outside the military academy's small circle. Even there, he was not recognized by many as a man with greatness in his future.

If Grant was an unpromising cadet when he arrived at West Point, Jackson had looked hopeless. An awkward country boy from the hills of western Virginia, he caused hysterics among the upper classmen when they saw his homespun clothes and coarse wool hat and the pair of saddlebags stained with horse sweat hanging from his rounded shoulders.

An orphan, Jackson's learning scarcely qualified him for a grammar school diploma. But the entrance examination for the military academy was a fairly simple test. The hard part was the course itself. One upper classman noted Jackson's "cold bright grey eyes" and remarked, "That fellow looks like he has come to stay."

The same cadet, a fellow Virginian, offered Jackson his hand in friendship. Jackson barely responded. His manner was surly and withdrawn. He was too unsure of himself to be friendly with anyone. The upper classman returned to his tent and announced: "In my opinion, Cadet Jackson of Virginia is a jackass."

The gaunt hillbilly soon impressed the entire corps, however, with his determination to survive. Jackson kept a notebook in which he wrote mottos and sayings to keep up his morale. The one he counted on most was "You may be whatever you resolve to be." He lived by those words, wrote one of his biographers, "as a scientist follows a formula.

He assumed literally that he could be what he resolved to be—by concentration, strain, sweat, endurance."

Night after night, Jackson studied into the dawn. He piled coal high on his grate just before lights out at ten o'clock. After taps, he stretched out on the floor in the firelight and dug at mathematical problems. The very terms were a puzzle to him. When he began the course, he had never even heard of fractions.

His academic misery touched the heart of one upper-class cadet, who began to tutor him privately. Other cadets never forgot Jackson's struggles. He would stand at the blackboard, his face wet with perspiration, the chalk dust spreading over his uniform. He literally fought his way through every recitation. Almost always he ended among the "immortals"—the tailenders of the class. But he survived, standing fifty-first among eight-three members of his class, in June.

The following year, still studying by midnight firelight, Jackson edged up into the middle of his class; by the time he reached the end of his first year, he stood seventeenth. Several cadets remarked that if the course had been two years longer, Jackson would have graduated at the head of the class.

Jackson finally made friends, too, his frosty reserve thawing as his confidence grew. He preferred cadets from classes behind him, which was not a common practice. They had to share his fondness for long walks and talks on serious subjects. If anyone in the corps was sick or in trouble, Tom Jackson was among the first to offer help. But there was a stern side to him, which was sometimes shocking.

One day Jackson found his musket gone and another gun in its place. The replacement was unpolished and dirty. Jackson had marked his musket so he could identify it. With the help of a cadet officer, he soon discovered the thief. Jackson demanded that he be court martialed and insisted on testifying against him. He wanted him discharged from the military academy. Only pleas from his classmates persuaded him to settle for a lighter punishment.

After graduation, Jackson went on to Mexico with Sam Grant and many others. Jackson arrived in time to participate in the climactic assault on

Mexico City. One of the strong points was the fortress of Chapultepec. Jackson, an artillery officer, advanced one of his guns to a point where he was dueling the Mexican batteries on the north side of the fortress, while a regiment of infantry also blazed away at him.

In a few minutes, all of Jackson's horses and half of his gunners were dead or wounded. The rest of his men dove into ditches beside the road. Jackson strolled up and down in the hail of lead, urging them to come back. "There's no danger. See, I'm not hit," he shouted.

An excited general rode up and ordered him to retreat. The young lieutenant gave him an argument. He said it would be less dangerous to stay where he was. He asked the general for fifty men to storm a barricade on the road ahead of them. As they argued, cheers floated down from the heights of Chapultepec. A young West Pointer named George E. Pickett ran up the Stars and Stripes on the flagstaff. The fortress had surrendered.

In 1851, Jackson retired from the army to teach at Virginia Military Institute. He was appalled at the outbreak of the Civil War, describing it as "the sum of all evils." But he felt his loyalty lay with Virginia. When she seceded, he marched to Richmond with his cadets and accepted a commission as a colonel of infantry.

Further south, another West Pointer reacted to the news of the coming war with even more dismay. Ohio-born William Tecumseh Sherman was serving as head of Louisiana's military school. A graduate of the class of 1840, "Cump" Sherman was never a model West Pointer. His keen mind had no difficulty with the mathematics and engineering courses, and he stood fourth in his class academically. But the 380 demerits he amassed in four years reduced his standing to sixth.

Reminiscing about Sherman in later years, a classmate said: "He was always ready for a lark and usually he had a grease spot on his pants from night feasts [in his room]. He was the best hash maker at West Point. We stole boiled potatoes in handkerchiefs and thrust them under our vests; we poked butter into our gloves and fastened them with forks to the underside of the table until we could smuggle them out of the dining room. We stole bread and when we got together at night 'Old Cump' would mix everything into hash and cook it on the stew pan over the fire. We ate it hot on toasted bread. We told stories and at this too Sherman was the best."

Not once was Sherman chosen to be a cadet officer—a post which always went to the most military cadets in the corps. Yet West Point made its mark on him in other ways. Writing to Ellen Ewing, the girl who would later become his wife, he criticized a cadet who was planning to resign and study law. "I would rather be a blacksmith. The nearer we come to that dreadful epoch, graduation day, the higher opinion I conceive of the duties and life of an officer of the United States Army. Think of that!"

Sherman spent most of his military career in the South. Among his closest friends were southern soldiers, particularly Braxton Bragg of North Carolina and George H. Thomas of Virginia. When a Louisiana friend told Sherman that South Carolina and other states had seceded, he burst into tears. He called the South's plunge into war "folly, madness, a crime against civilization." He was horrified that it would make him fight "against your people, whom I love the best."

Then Sherman the soldier began to prophesy. "You people speak so lightly of war. You don't know what you are talking about. War is a terrible thing. I know you are a brave fighting people but for every day of actual fighting there are months of marching, exposure and suffering. More men die in war from sickness than are killed in battle.

"You mistake too the people of the North. They are a peaceable people and an earnest people and will fight too. They are not going to let this country be destroyed without a mighty effort to save it.

"Besides, where are your men and appliances of war to contend against them! The North can make a steam engine, locomotive or railway car. Hardly a yard of cloth or a pair of shoes can you make. You are rushing into war with one of the most powerful, ingeniously mechanical, determined people on earth—right at your doors. You are bound to fail. Only in your spirit and determination are you prepared for war. In all else you are unprepared—and a bad cause to start with."

Sherman corresponded with Braxton Bragg about the war. Bragg was like Tom Jackson—severe and unhumorous, a man with a tense soul. Bragg wrote candidly to the friend of his West Point youth. When Sherman told him he was going to offer his services to the North, Bragg replied, "You are acting on a conviction of duty to yourself and to your family and friends. A similar duty on my part may throw us into an apparent hostile attitude but it is too terrible to contemplaté and I will not discuss it.

"You see the course of events—the union is already dissolved. The only question is can we reconstruct any government without bloodshed? I do not think we can—a few old political hacks and barroom bullies are leading public opinion."

Year later, Sherman said, "I think I knew Bragg as well as any living man. His heart was never in the Rebel cause." Appointed commander-in-chief of Louisiana's military forces, Bragg learned that Sherman's military school had a valuable arsenal needed to store the state's guns.

Realizing this might make Sherman look disloyal to northern observers, Bragg wrote to his friend to assure him that he would hire a man to care for the guns. Mournfully, Bragg added: "I shall continue to hope, though without reason, that Providence will yet avert the great evil. But should the worst come we shall still be personal friends."

A few days later, Bragg and five hundred soldiers seized federal forts in Louisiana and sent captured muskets to Sherman's arsenal. Sherman called the move an act of war and "a breach of common decency." He resigned as commander of the state's military academy. "I prefer to maintain my allegiance to the Constitution as long as a fragment of it survives," he told Louisiana's governor.

George Thomas, Sherman's best friend from West Point, underwent a different kind of agony. On March 12, 1861, he refused an offer from the governor of Virginia to become the state's chief of artillery. Thomas's two sisters were secessionists. They wrote him impassioned pleas to come home and serve the southern cause.

Unlike Lee and Jackson, Thomas had cut his ties to Virginia. In twenty-five years since he entered West Point in 1836, he had spent less than eighteen months with his southern relatives. His wife was from Troy, New York.

For Thomas, his West Point education was a gift from his country. That idea determined his loyalty.

"Turn every way he would, the one thing was uppermost—his duty to the government of the United States," his wife later recalled.

An angry Virginia government confiscated Thomas's property and his sisters banished him from the family forever. Until their deaths, they refused to permit the name George Henry Thomas to be mentioned in their home. They declared they had no such brother.

One would think that a man who resisted such pressures would be considered loyal. But Thomas's Virginia birth made him suspect to many northerners. Other West Pointers became generals in command of volunteers. But Thomas only replaced Lee as colonel of the 2nd Calvary, operating in the countryside around Washington, D.C., and for a while it looked as if he would remain a calvary colonel for the rest of the war.

Thomas had no politicians lobbying for him in Congress or at the White House, while northern-born soldiers had them by the dozen. But "Cump" Sherman, already a brigadier general, did not forget his classmate. Sherman was about to leave Washington with Robert Anderson, hero of Fort Sumter, to raise a Union army in Kentucky and Tennessee. When Sherman urged him to bring Thomas along and promote him to brigadier general as well, Anderson hesitated. Too many officers of the 2nd Cavalry had resigned and gone south.

Sherman vowed that he would stake his reputation on Thomas's loyalty. Convinced, Anderson persuaded a hesitant Lincoln to make Thomas a brigadier. Sherman rode into the country and found the 2nd Cavalry's camp, where he told his old friend the news. "Tom, you're a brigadier general," he said.

Thomas seldom got excited about anything. Now, he did not even smile. For a moment Sherman was assailed by doubts. Was the gossip about Thomas's disloyalty true after all? Sherman watched while Thomas mounted his horse. "Where are you going?" Sherman asked.

"I'm going south," Thomas said.

"My God, Tom," roared Sherman. "You've put me in a hell of a spot. I just made myself responsible for your loyalty."

"Give yourself no trouble, Billy," Thomas said. "I'm going south at the head of my troops."

8

Farewells East and West

At army posts around the nation, telegrams reported the bombardment against Fort Sumter. Virginian Dabney H. Maury of the class of 1846 was at Fort Staunton, deep in Indian territory. "It was some time before we could grasp the details," he recalled in his memoirs. "One after another we took the sheet and tried to read aloud its contents and each voice, broken with emotion in the effort, refused to do its owner's bidding.

"It was in no light or unappreciative mood that we sat looking at each other in the silence which followed the reading of the telegram; for we realized the greatness of the sacrifice expected of us, and it was with sad hearts that we turned our backs upon the friends and associations of the happy past and faced the issues of a future which had little to offer us save a consciousness of duty loyally performed."

Perhaps the saddest of these partings occurred in the little adobe town of Los Angeles, California. Tall, handsome Captain Winfield Scott Hancock and his wife, Almira, invited southerners to a farewell dinner. Among the guests were George Pickett and Dick Garnett, old friends from West Point and Mexican days, and Lewis Armistead, who had failed to graduate with the class of 1837 but had joined the army anyway and won three promotions for bravery in Mexico.

Pickett was an excitable, romantic soldier, fond of wearing his hair in long ringlets, yet courageous in battle. Although he was Virginia born, he had gotten his appointment to West Point by moving to Illinois, where a cousin had persuaded a congressman named Abraham Lincoln to send him to the military academy. Lincoln had followed his protégé's career closely, writing him letters of advice and encouragement, both of which Pickett needed.

Pickett rebelled against West Point's discipline. Swarms of demerits and a poor performance in the classroom left him at the foot of the class of 1846.

But he had proven himself a fighting soldier in Mexico.

As for Armistead, soldiering was in his blood. His uncle had commanded Baltimore's Fort McHenry on that famous night when the red glare of British rockets had inspired Francis Scott Key to write "The Star-Spangled Banner." Both he and Dick Garnett were opposed to secession. But they could not refuse when "Old Virginia" called them to its defense.

The evening in the Hancocks' quarters was full of suppressed emotion. Everyone tried to conceal their true feelings behind smiles and jokes. As midnight approached, one of the officers asked his wife to play some of their favorite songs. She sat down at the piano and began "Kathleen Mavourneen," a plaintive song about parting. "It may be for years, it may be forever," she sang.

Armistead looked across the room at Hancock. Tears ran down the Virginian's face as he thought of the days when together they had stormed Mexican barricades, fought Indians in the Florida Everglades, and crossed the plains and mountains from Kansas to California.

Armistead put his hands on Hancock's shoulders: "Hancock, goodbye. You can never know what this has cost me. I hope God will strike me dead if I am ever induced to leave my native soil should worse come to worst." He meant that he was prepared to defend Virginia, but he hoped he would never have to invade the North.

Turning to Almira Hancock, Armistead gave her a small satchel of mementos and personal items and asked her not to open it unless he was killed. In that case, he wanted her to keep his prayer book for herself. "By that time, there was not a dry eye in the party," Mrs. Hancock recalled.

In Philadelphia, John Pemberton, another West Pointer who had distinguished himself in Mexico, wrestled with emotions deeper than friendship. His mother and all the other members of his wealthy Pennsylvania family were siding with the Union. But Pemberton's heart was in the South, with his lovely dark-haired wife, Patty, whom he had met and married in Norfolk, Virginia.

Even in his cadet days, friends noticed that tall, serious John Pemberton was convinced of the justice of the southern cause. Yet he had everything to gain by staying with the North. A high rank in the Union army was virtually guaranteed him. His family made it clear that they would consider a decision to side with the South nothing less then treason.

As Pemberton argued with his family, his wife wrote him from Virginia: "My darling husband, why are you not with us? Jeff Davis has a post ready for you."

When Pemberton was ordered to duty in Washington, one of his brothers sat up all night with him on the train, making a last desperate effort to change his mind. A few weeks later, Pemberton was an officer in the Confederate army. Within a few months his two brothers became officers in the Union army.

Other West Pointers wrestled with the hard choice, which could only be made in the lonely world of the individual's conscience. Philip St. George Cook of Virginia chose the Union, although his own son joined the Confederate army and his daughter was married to Lee's favorite cadet, Jeb Stuart. Lee's problem cadet, Archibald Gracie, had gone into business in Mobile, Alabama, and he decided his loyalty lay with his adopted state.

A fiery Virginian, Powell Hill, debated with his old friend George McClellan before resigning to join the South. In earlier days, they had been rivals for the hand of blond, blue-eyed Nellie Marcy, one of the capital's reigning belles in the 1850s.

Miss Marcy might have preferred Hill, but her parents persuaded her to choose McClellan, who had become a prosperous railroad executive. When the war began, McClellan returned to the army as a general. For a time, hard feelings over Nellie had soured his friendship with Hill, but now they thought of West Point days and parted with regret.

"Hill, I am truly sorry you are going to leave us," McClellan told him. "But to be frank, I cannot blame you. If I were in your place I would do as you are about to do; but I am an Ohioan and I will stand by my state, too."

All told, 286 West Pointers, including 19 of northern birth, chose the Confederacy. Unfortunately, politicians in Washington were not inclined to give each man the right to make his own choice. Secretary of War Simon Cameron called the resignations "extraordinary treachery" and declared that the South's rebellion could never have reached "formidable proportions" without the help it was receiving from West Pointers. The angry secretary wondered if there was a "radical defect" in West Point's education.

Cameron was one of many Americans still devoted to the minuteman myth—the idea that all a nation needed to win a war was spirit and courage. In the overheated politics of Washington, D.C., he found many politicians who agreed with him. One wing of the Republican Party, known as Radicals, called for the abolition of the military academy.

This attitude filled the mind of more than one West Pointer with a sense of impending doom. If the politicians used the academy's graduates as whipping boys, the war was as good as lost. They felt the critics were ignoring how many southern-born West Pointers had remained loyal to the Union—an impressive total of 162, including six men from South Carolina, where secession fever burned hottest.

In the South, with West Pointer Jefferson Davis as president, there was no hesitation about appointing graduates to important commands. The North clung to the aging generals who had won victories in Mexico. But in army camps throughout the North, West Pointers of lower rank, such as Sam

Grant, were hard at work molding an army out of civilians who had volunteered at Lincoln's call.

Elsewhere, West Pointers were forseeing the strategy of the war. One day, Cump Sherman invited his brother, Senator John Sherman, to have dinner with him and George Thomas, who was still in the Maryland countryside with his 2nd Cavalry regiment. Spreading a map on the floor of a country tavern, Thomas and Sherman placed a dot on Richmond, Virginia, as target number one of the Union armies. Then they turned their eyes to the West, and marked the cities of Knoxville, Chattanooga, and Nashville, Tennessee, and Vicksburg, Mississippi, as crucial to both sides.

Years later, writing his memoirs, Senator Sherman marveled that the two professional soldiers were able to "confidently and correctly" predict where many of the war's greatest battles would be fought. Stranger still, they were destined to be "leading actors" in these battles, which they foresaw like prophets of the god of war years before they took place.

9

Brothers in Battle

In Braintree, Massachusetts, the man who
was known as the father of West Point,
former Superintendent Sylvanus Thayer, made a
gloomy prediction. The side that advanced first
would be defeated and "the greater the number of
the advancing forces, the more certain would be
their defeat." Like other West Pointers, he regarded
the war as a disaster. But as a man of the North, he
supported the Union. Thayer hoped that the Union
army would wait until they were thoroughly trained
and equipped before they invaded the South.

Thayer's advice was ignored. The politicians in
Washington, D.C., and in the Confederate capital,
which had been moved to Richmond when Virginia

seceded, were in a hurry. Both sides envisioned a one-battle war. "On to Richmond" was the cry of amateur strategists such as Horace Greeley, editor of the influential *New York Tribune*.

The Union general Irwin McDowell invaded Virginia on July 18 with 30,000 men. His West Point classmate of 1838, Pierre G. T. Beauregard, met him at a small creek known as Bull Run. Neither general had ever directed an army in battle before. The result was one of the strangest encounters in the history of warfare: a Union victory in the morning, a Confederate triumph in the afternoon.

At a crucial moment in the battle, the brigade commanded by Tom Jackson repulsed a fierce Union assault. Another West Pointer, Bernard Bee, trying to rally his own men, cried: "Look, there's Jackson's men standing like a stone wall!" The nickname swept through the Confederate army. Henceforth, the gaunt brigadier general became Stonewall Jackson.

In those early days of the war, many southern West Pointers who had resigned from the regular army were still wearing scraps of their old Union uniforms. Jeb Stuart was particularly fond of a blue overcoat that had kept him warm during the years he spent as a cavalryman in Kansas. One day he was on outpost duty near the Union lines when he met a horseman in blue at a bend in the narrow road.

Stuart recognized him as Delavan Perkins of the class of 1849, who had taught him mathematics during his cadet days. He seemed to be alone and Stuart assumed he had joined the Confederates. "Howdy, Perk, glad to see you've come over. What's your command?" he called.

Around the bend in the road rumbled a battery of Union field artillery. Grinning, Perkins pointed to the guns. "Hello, Beauty," he said, using Stuart's West Point nickname. "How are you? That's my command."

"Oh, the devil," Stuart said and put spurs to his horse, quickly outdistancing the artillerymen, whose horses were pulling their cannon.

During the battle of Bull Run, Stuart used his blue great-coat as a daring disguise. Separated from his cavalrymen, he rode up to a company of Union infantry in a field, crouching behind a rail fence. "Take down those bars," Stuart shouted.

The soldiers obeyed. Stuart whipped out his sword, gestured to some nearby woods as if he was signalling a hidden regiment and said: "Throw down your arms. You're all dead men." The entire company dropped their guns, fell on their faces, and surrendered.

Not long after Bull Run, Stuart led a raid that drove back a Union force. Among them was Charles Griffin, another friend from West Point days. Griffin left behind a note with a local citizen before retreating.

Dear Beauty:

I have called to see you and regret very much that you were not in. Can't you dine with me at Willard's [a famous Washington hotel] tomorrow? Keep your "black horse" off me!

Stuart replied with a note that echoed the confidence southerners were feeling.

Dear Griffin:

I heard that you called and hastened to see you, but as soon as you saw me coming you were guilty of the discourtesy of turning your back on me. However, you probably hurried on to Washington to get the dinner ready. I hope to dine at Willard's, if not tomorrow, certainly before long.

> Yours to count on,
> Beauty

Fitzhugh Lee became one of Jeb Stuart's cavalry commanders. Some months later he decided to imitate Jeb's brash style. Fitz caught a Pennsylvania cavalry regiment unprepared and routed them. When he learned that the troops belonged to his West Point classmate, William W. Averell, he dashed off a note.

Dear Averell:

I wish you would put up your sword, leave my state and go home. You ride a good horse. I ride a better. Yours can beat mine running. Send me over a bag of coffee.

> Fitz

By this time, Union cavalrymen were ready to take on the reckless southern horsemen. Averell decided to pay Fitz a return visit. With five regiments behind him he stormed across the Rappahannock River and tore apart one of Fitz's outposts. Only desperate courage saved the rest of Fitz's smaller command from total defeat. Withdrawing, Averell left behind a sack of coffee and another note.

Dear Fitz:

Here's your coffee. Here's your call. How do you like it? How's that horse?

Averell

No West Pointer rose as rapidly in the Union Army as George McClellan. Called "McNapoleon" by his admirers, he soon became commander of the Union Army of the Potomac, the most powerful force in the East. Nevertheless, men such as George Pickett continued to think of him as a friend. When McClellan was laid low by a fever, Pickett wrote his fiancée: "I've heard my dear old friend McClellan is lying ill about ten miles from here. May some loving, soothing hand minister to him. He was, he is, he always will be, even were his pistol pointed at my heart, my dear loved friend."

Powell Hill had meanwhile become a Confederate major general. His division was soon famed for ferocious attacks. Hill seemed to take special pleasure in frustrating McClellan's battle plans and Union soldiers became convinced that Hill was still angry about losing the beautiful Nellie Marcy to his Yankee friend.

Once, after beating off a series of Hill's attacks, the Union men were trying to get some rest. Blaring bugles and rattling musketry announced that Hill was back for another assault. "My God, Nellie," groaned one veteran as he pulled on his boots. "Why didn't you marry him?"

In spite of Hill, McClellan seemed to have victory in his grasp in 1862. His huge army crunched to within sight of Richmond's church steeples. The Confederate commander, Joseph Johnston, seemed powerless to stop the Union drive. A worried Jefferson Davis rode out with Robert E. Lee, who was serving as his military advisor. Davis was dismayed to see Johnston being carried off the field, badly wounded. His second in command confessed he had no idea how to confront the Union assault that was certain to come tomorrow.

Davis turned to Lee. "I am putting you in command of this army," he said.

Within a week, Lee proved this was the best decision Jefferson Davis ever made. Seizing the initiative, the Virginian saved Richmond with a series of counteroffensives, known as the Seven Days' battles, that drove McClellan into humiliating retreat.

Henceforth, Robert E. Lee was the warrior chief of the Confederacy. Again and again, he checked and parried assaults of much bigger Union armies. In these same months, Stonewall Jackson emerged as Lee's daring lieutenant.

The strategic diversion Jackson created in the Shenandoah Valley in the spring of 1862 is considered one of the most brilliant campaigns in military history. With never more than 17,000 men under his command, Jackson pinned down four times that many Union soldiers, badly needed by McClellan in his drive on Richmond. Marching his men at incredible speed at night or over back roads, Jackson repeatedly outwitted and defeated the baffled Union commanders, finally forcing them to evacuate the valley. Jackson then coolly withdrew his own army to join Lee in the Seven Days' battles that drove McClellan into retreat.

At the second battle of Bull Run in August 1862, Jackson marched fifty-four miles in two days, circling the Union Army to capture a huge supply dump at Manassas Junction. Before the battle of Chancellorsville in May 1863, Lee summoned him to his headquarters. They were facing a Union army of 130,000 men, twice the size of their army.

"General Jackson," Lee said, as they studied a map. "What do you propose to do?"

Jackson ran his finger along a forest road that led far around the Union Army to their rear. "Go around here," he said.

"What do you propose to make this movement with?"

"With my whole corps," Jackson said.

Lee permitted Jackson to vanish into the forest with half his army. For twenty-four hours Jackson's "foot cavalry," as some called them, followed "Old Stonewall" through the woods. Behind each regiment marched a guard with orders to bayonet anyone who tried to desert. Men collapsed from hunger and thirst, but Jackson pressed on until he emerged in the rear of the Union army the next day.

Relaxed Union soldiers were cooking their dinners. Jackson marshalled his men in the trees. At a nod from him, the southern bugles blew and waves of gray-uniformed Confederates charged, howling, to smash a third of the Union army to panicky fragments.

Through the darkness Jackson rode with his surging battalions, shouting, "Push forward, push forward." Total victory seemed near when a North Carolina regiment, mistaking Jackson and his staff for Union cavalry in the gloom, fired on him, killing two of his aides and fatally wounding the general. From that moment, the fury flickered out of the southern attack, and the Union army escaped to fight another day.

When Jackson died a week later, a shudder of foreboding went through the South. "I have lost my right arm," Lee said.

Years later, a clergyman who spoke at the unveiling of a statue of Jackson said: "When in Thy inscrutable wisdom, O Lord, Thou didst ordain that the Confederacy should fall, then didst Thou find it necessary to remove thy servant, Stonewall Jackson. Amen."

To this day, many southerners remain convinced that if Stonewall Jackson had lived, the South would have won the war.

10

The Quiet Man Front and Center

While Robert E. Lee and Stonewall Jackson humbled the Union army in the East, a different story unfolded in the West. The drama revolved around the quiet man, Ulysses S. Grant. Before the war was a year old, Grant electrified the nation with his capture of Fort Donelson on the Cumberland River in Tennessee.

To win this victory, Grant violated a supposedly unbreakable military rule. He besieged a fort with more men in it than he had in his army. He did it by boldly bluffing the southerners into surrender by convincing them he had an overwhelming force under his command. The general who surrendered

15,000 men to him was his old West Point friend, Simon Bolivar Buckner.

After the surrender, Grant thought of the day he arrived in New York broke and Buckner had loaned him money. Without a word, Grant stuffed a roll of greenbacks into Buckner's hands and walked away.

A few months later, on April 6, 1862, Grant's army was attacked without warning at Shiloh, Mississippi, by a superior Confederate force. At first, the Union lines buckled and then broke. Yet Grant revealed the unshakeable calm that his West Point classmates had seen. With half his army shattered, he withdrew the rest into a grim semicircle with their backs to the Tennessee River. They fought off repeated Confederate assaults until night fell.

At one point, a hysterical Union officer rushed up to Grant and begged him to retreat across the river. Grant looked surprised. The thought had never occurred to him. "Retreat?" he said. "Oh, no. We are all right now. Tomorrow we will drive them."

The next day, that is exactly what happened. The Confederate army retreated before Grant's counter-attacks.

At Shiloh, William Tecumseh Sherman fought brilliantly as one of Grant's subordinate generals. It was the beginning of a remarkable partnership between these two very different men. Many people were puzzled by the way Sherman accepted Grant's leadership. They did not understand that West Point had trained both men to emphasize results, not personality. Sherman saw that Grant had an uncanny ability to produce the one result that counted—victory.

Once, in a talkative moment, Sherman told another officer why Grant was his superior. "I'm a damn sight smarter than Grant. I know more about organization, supply and administration and about everything else than he does. But I'll tell you where he beats me and where he beats the world. He don't care a damn for what the enemy does out of his sight, but it scares *me* like hell."

After the battle of Shiloh, Grant was criticized in the press for his heavy casualties. Politicians did their best to discredit him. He was temporarily removed from command of the western army, and Sherman heard he was on the brink of resigning. For a more selfish man, this might have been good news. Sherman stood a fair chance of getting Grant's job.

Instead, Sherman wrote letters to newspapers, angrily defending Grant. Then he rode to his tent and asked him if it was true that he was leaving the army.

"Sherman," Grant said. "You know that I'm in the way here. I have stood it as long as I can."

"Where are you going?"

"St. Louis."

Have you any business there?"

"Not a bit in the world."

Sherman urged Grant to stay in the army no matter what the newspapers or anyone else said about him. Over and over, he told Grant that the army and the country needed him. For more than an hour Sherman talked and Grant listened.

The quiet man thanked Sherman and promised he would at least stay in camp and think it over. A week later, while Sherman was on a scouting expedition, he received a note from Grant—he had decided to stay with the army. Sherman immediately wrote him a letter of congratulations. It did not bother him in the least that he had talked himself out of a chance for promotion.

The major task of the Union armies in the West was to open the Mississippi so that goods and farm products from the western states could be shipped down the river to New Orleans for export. In this struggle, Sherman and Grant discovered a new kind of war. It was Grant, the slouchy, silent little man in the dusty field uniform, who found it first.

Marching to besiege Vicksburg, Mississippi, with Confederate armies threatening both his flanks, Grant received a jittery plea from Sherman to "stop all troops till your army is partially supplied with wagons."

Back from Grant came a startling reply. He had no intention of trying to maintain his army from the Union supply base. He would bring up rations of bread, coffee, and salt and "make the country furnish the balance."

The baffled Confederate generals, assuming Grant was fighting by the book, committed half their army to strike at his supply lines. Eighteen thousand Confederate soldiers floundered in his rear and found no supply lines to strike. Meanwhile, in front of Vicksburg, Grant was smashing the divided Confederates and driving them into the city in confusion.

The commander of the Vicksburg garrison was John Pemberton, the Pennsylvanian who resisted his family's pleas not to join the South. Watching his beaten army flee into the city's fortifications, where he knew they faced starvation and eventual surrender, Pemberton said to a friend: "Just thirty years ago I began my military career by receiving an appointment to the United States Military Academy, and today—the same date—my career is ended in disaster and disgrace."

Pemberton did everything in his power to defend Vicksburg. For three months he beat off attacks by Grant's superior army. Only when Pemberton's men were reduced to ragged skeletons, too weak to resist a final assault, did he surrender the fortress city on the Mississippi.

Under a small tree on July 4, 1863, John Pemberton and Sam Grant met to discuss surrender terms. Instead of marching the starved defenders to prison camps, where they would have died by the thousands, Grant paroled them all on the promise that they would fight no more.

Many embittered southeners thought Pemberton should have fought to his last man. There were ugly rumors about his loyalty and northern bribes. When Pemberton visited his family in Virginia a few weeks after the surrender, his children did not recognize him. His hair and beard had turned white.

After the war, Sam Grant came to Pemberton's defense. "A more conscientious, honorable man never lived," he said. "All the time he was in Vicksburg and I outside it, I knew he would hold on to the last."

11

Grant Men

M ost of the credit for the Vicksburg victory goes to Grant, who made the daring command decisions. But Grant made sure that he had some of West Point's smartest men on his staff. At the top of this list of young officers, who came to be known as "Grant men," was James Harrison Wilson, one of the brightest graduates of the class of 1860.

Wilson never hesitated to advise generals. At the battle of Antietam, Maryland, in 1862, he saw Major General Joe Hooker leaving the field with a foot wound. Wilson told him that he should return to the front line even if he had to be carried on a stretcher, "with his bugles blowing and his corps flag flying over him."

When George McClellan was relieved as commander of the Union army in the East, a friend advised him to ask for a lesser command in the West. McClellan haughtily replied that he would not consider anything less than commander in chief of all the armies, East and West. Wilson told him that if he were not offered an independent command, he should take a corps or a division in another army. Failing that, he should return home and raise a regiment. Failing that he should shoulder a musket and enlist as a private.

Not every general would put up with this kind of subordination. But Sam Grant saw that Wilson had both brains and gall, and used both in the Vicksburg campaign. He first proposed the idea of ferrying troops past the city's batteries with gunboats protecting the transports. South of the city, the troops were able to cross the Mississippi and attack Vicksburg from the rear.

When John McClernand, a politician who had wangled himself a general's stars, started a feud with Grant, Wilson ended it. He brought McClernand an order from Grant. It was answered by a volley of oaths. "General McClernand," said the twenty-six-year-old Wilson. "I am astonished by what you are saying. It seems to me that you are cursing me as much as you are cursing General Grant. If this is so, although you are a major general and I am only a lieutenant colonel, I will pull you off that horse and beat the boots off you."

McClernand apologized. He said he was not cursing, he was "simply expressing his intense feelings on the subject." This answer became a favorite joke at Grant's headquarters. Whenever Grant heard anyone cursing, he would reprimand him, then say he was sure the officer was just expressing his intense feelings on the subject.

Another gifted Grant man was James Birdseye McPherson, who had graduated from West Point at the head of the class of 1853. McPherson served as chief engineer under Grant at Fort Donelson and was at his side throughout the bloody battle of Shiloh. At Grant's suggestion, McPherson was made a brigadier general and became military superintendent of railroads in western Tennessee. He soon knew more about that vital stretch of country than any other officer in the Union army.

A handsome man with great personal charm, McPherson rose to major general, thanks again to Grant, and commanded the 17th Corps during the Vicksburg campaign. He soon had Sherman saying: "If he lives he'll out-distance Grant and myself."

William Farrar "Baldy" Smith of the class of 1845 helped Grant rescue another Union army from a disaster that might have lost the war. In September, 1863, Grant was ordered to take command of one of the main western armies, the army of the Cumberland, which the Confederates, under Braxton Bragg, had driven behind the breastworks guarding Chattanooga.

By the time Grant and Smith arrived, the army's situation was desperate. The men were living on half rations and had barely enough ammunition for another battle. Supplies reached them only by a wagon haul of sixty miles over the mountains. Entrenched in the hills above the city, the Confederates controlled every other route.

One day, Baldy Smith took a horseback ride along the bank of the Tennessee River. At a crossing known as Brown's Ferry, he spent two hours studying the opposite shore and the hills above it. When Smith returned to headquarters, he had a plan to break the siege. His trained eye had seen how the Union army could lunge across the river at the crossing and seize the south side of the river and the hills, which were lightly defended.

Grant instantly approved the plan. That night, Smith threw a 1,350-foot pontoon bridge across the river. Grant poured thousands of men onto the south shore in a few hours. The stunned Confederates fell back in confusion. Within five days, a flood of supplies was pouring down the road from Nashville to restore the half-starved army of the Cumberland. A few weeks later, Grant led them forward to a series of victories that swept the unlucky Braxton Bragg and the Confederates out of Tennessee.

12

None But the Brave

On both sides of the battle lines young West Pointers won praise and promotion. Jeb Stuart's exploits as a cavalry commander rapidly elevated him to the status of a legend. Twice he and his brigade circled the entire Union army while it was commanded by George McClellan, shooting up outposts, tearing up rail lines, and giving the general nervous spasms. During the campaign that was climaxed by the second battle of Bull Run in August 1862, Stuart led 1500 horsemen on another daring raid that overran the Union army's headquarters, capturing staff officers and papers that gave General Lee invaluable information. Always a joker, Stuart also carried off a uniform belonging to the Union commander, John Pope. It was displayed in the window of a store on the main street of Richmond for several days. After another raid, in which he captured tons of federal ammunition and supplies, he sent a telegram to the Union quartermaster general in Washington, D.C., complaining that the Union mules were of poor quality and could barely haul away his loot.

Another young West Pointer who seized the imagination of the South was John Pelham. A captain of horse artillery in Jeb Stuart's cavalry, he won several citations for bravery. At the battle of Fredericksburg, Virginia, Pelham held up the Union advance for hours, duelling their massed batteries with a single light gun. Watching him, Robert E. Lee exclaimed: "Is it not glorious to see such courage in one so young?"

Soon the "gallant Pelham" became an everyday phrase. George Armstrong Custer, rising rapidly as a Union cavalryman, sent a message through the lines: "I rejoice, dear Pelham, in your success." Another Union graduate explained this attitude to a friend. "I'm not disloyal when I tell you we heard with secret pride of his gallant deeds. It was what we had the right to expect of him—he was one of the best of us."

Early on March 17, 1863, Pelham joined his West Point friends Tam Rosser, Jeb Stuart, and Fitzhugh Lee, at Kelly's Ford on the Rappahannock River. They were trying to repel a raid by Union cavalry. Normally, Pelham stayed in the rear, directing the fire of his guns. That day he was returning from a visit to a young lady, and his battery was not on the field. He decided to join the cavalry in a charge. Drawing his saber, he rode to the head of a column of the Third Virginia Regiment and shouted, "Forward!"

An instant later, a shell burst overhead. Pelham toppled from his horse. His eyes were open, his lips wide in a smile. But blood trickled from the back of his head. A shell fragment had pierced his brain. His friends rushed him to the nearest doctor, but Pelham was dead. When Jeb Stuart heard the news, he bowed his head on his horse's neck and wept. Many other veterans joined him.

On the northern side, Custer began to match the daring of Stuart, Lee, and other southern cavalrymen. Again and again, he found himself charging horsemen commanded by Tam Rosser. Once, while Custer's men were on the defensive, expecting a Southern attack, they saw Rosser emerge from some trees and ride boldly within range of Union sharpshooters. He threw back his grey cape, revealing a red lining, offering them an even better target.

Custer hastily ordered the sharpshooters to hold their fire. The next day he sent a message to Rosser under a flag of truce. "Tam, do not expose yourself so. Yesterday I could have killed you."

After the battle of Williamsburg, Virginia, in May 1862, Custer found another rebel classmate, John "Gimlet" Lea, lying wounded in a barn. Custer arranged for Lea to be carried to the home of a Mrs. Durfey in Williamsburg. During his recuperation, Lea fell in love with her daughter, and they became engaged.

Custer received permission to pay Lea a visit. The Union army, abandoning the drive on Richmond from the Yorktown peninsula, was withdrawing to Washington. Lea should have been happy to hear this piece of news. Instead, he was downcast. He wanted Custer to be the best man at his wedding.

Always ready for a party, Custer agreed—if they could arrange to have the wedding the next day.

In a letter to his sister, Custer described the ceremony. Lea was dressed in "a bright new Rebel uniform trimmed with gold lace." Custer wore his "full uniform of blue." The bride's cousin was her maid of honor. She burst into tears at the end of the ceremony. Teasing her, Lea suggested she was in love with Custer and urged her to marry him.

Custer spent the next two weeks at the Durfey house, letting Cousin Maggie play and sing southern songs for him, and otherwise try to woo him into changing sides. Meanwhile, Custer played cards with Lea, letting him win every time.

Shortly after Custer became a brigadier general, he announced he would not cut his hair until he entered Richmond. He kept his word until his hair was hanging a foot long over his shoulders in golden curls. His West Point roommate, Tully McCrae, described Custer in August 1863. He was wearing a velveteen suit covered with gold braid and topped with a huge collar on which he pinned his general's stars. It was definitely not the regulation uniform of the U.S. Army. But in a war, the army often allows soldiers to dress as they please, if they fight well. Tully McCrae insisted that Custer was not a show-off, in spite of his uniform. Many people thought he strutted and bragged too much. But his fellow West Pointers were never among the critics. For them, the strutting and the flamboyant uniforms were simply part of being Custer.

James Wilson, the Grant man who was quick to criticize generals, was obviously thinking of Custer when he wrote in his memoirs: "The modest man is not always the best soldier. Some of the best, while shamelessly singing their own praises, were brave, dashing and enterprising to an unusual degree."

Perhaps the best glimpse of Custer's daring and wild humor came in the Shenandoah Valley. It was also the climax of his rivalry with Tam Rosser. Beside a stream known as Tom's Brook, Rosser posted his men and waited for the Union attack. Custer chose Rosser's position as his special target. He rode forward until he was within easy range of Confederate sharpshooters. Then he swept his broad-brimmed hat from his head and led his division in a headlong charge.

Rosser's line broke and Custer chased him for ten miles in what Union men called "the Woodstock races." Custer captured Rosser's supply train and wagons, some of which contained trunks of clothes. The next day, Custer pranced out of his headquarters wearing Rosser's dress uniform, which was six sizes too big for him. Under a flag of truce he sent Tam another note, asking him to be sure his tailor made the jacket shorter the next time.

13

The Saddest Day

Most of the time, there were more tears than laughter in West Point's confrontations across the battle lines. Nowhere was this truer than at the battle of Gettysburg. There, on July 3, 1863, after two days of bloody combat, Robert E. Lee chose to make a climactic assault on the center of the Union lines, on a hill called Missionary Ridge.

Major General George Pickett was placed in charge of the attack. Among his brigadier generals were Richard Garnett, who dragged himself from a sickbed, shivering with fever, and Lewis Armistead. Commanding the Union troops huddled behind the stone walls at the top of the ridge was Major General Winfield Scott Hancock. Did these old friends think of that farewell party in Los Angeles, two years ago? Did Armistead in particular recall his words about leaving his native soil?

Gettysburg was in Pennsylvania. Robert E. Lee had decided to invade the North to force Lincoln to negotiate peace. Armistead was not the only man in the Confederate army who disliked the idea. As long as the South fought on the defensive, they could claim the North was attacking them. But Armistead was a soldier. So swallowing his doubts, he obeyed orders and marched his brigade of Pickett's division into line for the attack.

On the crest of Missionary Ridge, Hancock rode along the entire front of his command to reassure his jittery men. The Union army in the East had broken and run too often in the face of a Confederate charge. Lee's artillery was laying down a terrific barrage. Shells shrieked past Hancock on his big horse. One of his aides begged him not to expose himself so recklessly. The men in his corps were depending on his leadership.

"There are times when the life of a corps commander doesn't count," Hancock replied.

As the artillery's battering ceased, out of the woods swept the southern brigades. Too sick to walk, Dick Garnett rode his horse at the head of his brigade. Brigadier General Lewis Armistead strode not far away. He put his black slouch hat on the point of his sword so his men could keep track of him.

Hancock's men raked them with artillery, but the Confederates came steadily on. As they mounted the ridge, Hancock sent Union regiments swarming down the southern flanks to hurl blasts of musketry at them, a tactic known as enfilading fire. Finally, a tremendous volley from the men on the ridge swept away whole ranks.

Dick Garnett fell, riddled by a dozen bullets. Untouched, Lewis Armistead strode into the gun-smoke. On the other side of the stone wall, artillery-man Alonzo Cushing, of the class of 1860, ignored a mortal wound to push his gun forward and fire a final blast into the charging Confederates. A few dozen feet away, Hancock toppled from his horse. A minié ball had smashed into his groin.

Armistead vaulted over the wall and paused there, his hand on the dying Cushing's cannon. The nearest

Union soldiers broke and ran. But on either side of them, the blue line stood firm. Swarms of reinforcements rushed to fill the gap left by the runaways. Armistead realized he was almost alone. Only a handful of his men had survived the carnage on the slope. Before he could give an order, a half dozen bullets cut him down.

As Hancock's men carried the dying Armistead to the rear, he asked for his old friend from Los Angeles and West Point days. They told him Hancock, too, was wounded and probably dying. Armistead wept. A few hours later he was dead. Hancock recovered from his wound.

Soon after the battle, Almira Hancock opened the suitcase Armistead had given her on their last night in Los Angeles. In the prayer book he had wanted her to keep was a soldier's motto: "Trust in God and fear nothing."

In this hour of terrible defeat, Robert E. Lee showed his greatness by taking full responsibility for the disaster. He could have blamed Pickett or the army's second in command, James Longstreet, who had opposed the attack and supported it half-heartedly with his men and guns.

Instead, Lee told everyone: "It is I who have lost this fight. You must help me out of it the best way you can." With their guns ready, the Confederates retreated to Virginia, daring the Union army to attack them. The Union commander decided his army was too badly mauled to risk it.

Back in Virginia, Lee told Jefferson Davis he was ready to resign his command. Davis would not even consider the idea. But the Confederacy had suffered a mortal blow. Never again could Lee take the offensive.

Ulysses Grant soon came East, and Abraham Lincoln handed over to him full charge of the war. Grant's approach was brutally simple. "It is my design to work all parts of the army together towards a common end," he said. He proceeded to weave a ring of fire around the dying Confederacy.

14

The Fighting Irishman

When Grant came East he brought another West Pointer with him. His name was Phil Sheridan. Robert E. Lee may have dimly remembered him from his years as a superintendent. Sheridan had caused a fair share of the gray hairs on Lee's head.

From his first day at the military academy, the stumpy, bandy-legged Ohioan was in trouble. The flowing vertical lines of the cadet uniform looked strange on his 5'5" physique. He was Irish in an era when hundreds of thousands of fellow Celts were pouring into the United States, arousing sharp anti-immigrant feelings among Americans. In every one of his cadet years, Sheridan came close to being expelled for demerits, most of them collected for fighting someone who had made a nasty crack about the Irish.

His worst brawl was with Cadet Sergeant William R. Terrill. A Virginian with a haughty manner, Terrill gave Sheridan an order on the parade ground one September afternoon in a tone of voice Sheridan thought "improper." The order was to "dress"—to line up more exactly with the cadets to the right and left. Sheridan said he was perfectly dressed already. Terrill said something about an Irishman not having enough brains to know whether he was dressed. Sheridan lowered his musket, with a bayonet attached, and charged.

Terrill managed to dodge Sheridan's first lunge and then ran for his life. Sheridan did not chase him. He realized he had made a very serious mistake. Only mutiny was worse than threatening a superior officer with bodily harm.

Terrill put Sheridan on report. The next time Sheridan saw him, Sheridan swung for his jaw. Bigger and heavier than Sheridan, Terrill started giving Sheridan a terrific beating. A tactical officer caught them and put them both on report.

Sheridan was in the wrong both times. An average cadet probably would have been expelled. But the tactical officers knew what Sheridan had been going through for two years. They went to Superintendent Lee and persuaded him not to expel Sheridan. Instead, he was suspended for a year.

When Sheridan returned to West Point, he went right back to fighting anyone who even came close to insulting him. At graduation he was within five demerits of expulsion. Some say he had gone over the 200 demerit limit, but the tactical officers again persuaded Superintendent Lee to make an exception.

A comparatively old lieutenant when the war began, Sheridan at first got stuck in army administration, working as a quartermaster gathering supplies. When he finally persuaded the government to give him command of a cavalry regiment, his rise was meteoric. Within thirty-five days he became a brigadier general in the western army.

The night before the battle of Perryville, Kentucky, in October 1862, Sheridan was stalking around the Union campfires. Suddenly he saw a familiar face across the dancing flames. It was William Terrill. After a bitter quarrel with his Virginia father, Terrill had chosen to stay with the Union. He too was a brigadier general.

Since the day Sheridan almost bayonetted him, they had never spoken. They stared across the fire for a silent moment. Terrill held out his hand. Sheridan took it in his tough grip. They sat down and reminisced about cadet days.

The next afternoon, in the middle of the battle, Terrill tried to rally his men after they had retreated in confusion before a Confederate charge. A southern bullet cut him down. He died that night.

Terrill's brother, a graduate of Virginia Military Insitute, fought for the South. He became one of Lee's brigadier generals. A year later, he was killed fighting one of Grant's attacks. After the war the grieving father buried them side by side with a single tombstone over them. On it he carved their names and identical ranks in the rival armies. Under that, he placed a single line: "God alone knows which was right."

Sheridan swiftly became one of Lincoln's favorite generals. Men would follow this fighting Irishman anywhere. At Look-out Mountain in Tennessee, his troops had to fight their way up an almost vertical slope. Sheridan whipped out a silver flask and raised it to a Confederate officer on the crest. "Here's to you," he shouted and took a long swallow.

The Confederate replied with a volley from six cannon that almost blew off Sheridan's head. Brushing dirt from his eyes, Sheridan growled, "That's damn ungenerous. I'll take those guns for that!" With a bellow he led his men up the mountain in an irresistible charge.

Sheridan's finest hour was the battle of Winchester, in the Shenandoah Valley of Virginia. Assigned to clear this vital territory of Confederate troops, Sheridan quickly routed the southern army under Jubal Early. But West Pointer Early was a shrewd, resourceful soldier. He scratched together his battered regiments and waited until the Union army lowered its guard. In a dawn attack, he routed them in turn.

Sheridan was fourteen miles away when Early struck on September 19, 1864. Within minutes, Sheridan was on his big black horse, Rienzi, riding toward the sound of the guns. Soon he met thousands of his soldiers running down the pike road, apparently with no plans to stop until they got to

Washington, D.C. The sight of Sheridan changed their minds.

One Vermont private told his parents what he saw and heard: "Sheridan was about fifty yards in advance of his bodyguard with his hat in his hand shouting 'Come to the front with me, boys, and we will make this matter all right.'"

"It was an awful moment," the Vermont private said. "But everybody and everything followed Sheridan."

An aide described how Sheridan, "without slowing from a gallop, pointed to the front. Men cheered and shouldered arms and started back. As he galloped on, his features gradually grew set, as though carved in stone. The same dull red glint I had seen in his black eyes when the battle was going against us was there now."

Onto the chaotic battlefield Sheridan rode. He jumped a fence manned by Union skirmishers and drove his exhausted horse up a little hill between his men and the southerners. Disregarding enemy bullets, he rode on to inspire other units.

An infantry colonel shouted to him: "The army is whipped."

Sheridan snarled: "You are, but the army isn't."

Up and down the line he rode while behind him rose a roar of Union men returning by the thousands. "We're going to get a twist on these fellows," Sheridan shouted. "We're going to lick them out of their boots."

In poems and stories about his ride from Winchester, Sheridan led his men forward in a headlong rush, minutes after he arrived on the battlefield. Actually, he spent from 10:30 A.M. until 4 P.M. unscrambling regiments and divisions, bringing up artillery, feeling out the Confederates' strength. At 4 P.M. Sheridan sent a coordinated army forward, infused with driving fury. They smashed into the Confederate line "at a double quick with screams of delight and triumph."

The outnumbered Confederates fled. Sheridan seemed to be everywhere at once, lashing his men into pursuit. He found a group of infantrymen floundering behind the advance. "We can't run. We're all tuckered out," they gasped.

"If you can't run then shoot and holler," Sheridan roared. "We've got the damndest twist on them you ever saw."

The Confederate defeat became a rout. For more three miles their ambulances, artillery wagons, and supply wagons littered the road down which they fled. The next day Grant wrote to Secretary of War Edwin Stanton that the battle at Winchester stamped Sheridan "what I always thought him, one of the ablest of generals."

Lincoln remarked that he had always thought a cavalryman ought to be about 6'4", "but now five feet five inches seems about right."

Around the campfire on the night of victory, Sheridan told his officers, "I'm going to get much more credit for this than I deserve. Had I been here in the morning, the same thing would have taken place and had I not returned the same thing would have taken place."

Not a man who had spent five minutes on the battlefield agreed with him. It was Sheridan who had turned defeat into victory.

15
The Fiery Circle

In Ulysses S. Grant's first drive toward Richmond, Virginia, in the spring of 1864, he lost 15,000 men fighting Robert E. Lee in the tangled forest called The Wilderness. Everyone expected him to withdraw north of the Potomac River to regroup. Glumly, the blue-clad soldiers trudged along roads familiar from a dozen earlier retreats.

Then they came to a crossroads. They could not believe their eyes. The regiments ahead of them were turning south! A tremendous cheer burst from the lips of every man in the column. For the first time they felt the presence of a general who fought to win.

Again and again, Grant hammered at Lee's army, taking fearful casualties, but costing the Confederates almost as many men. Northern newspapers howled for Grant's resignation. They called him "the Butcher." But Grant insisted he was shortening the war in the only way a war could be shortened. Ignoring his critics, he studied his maps and moved south, always south.

"I propose to fight it out on this line if it takes all summer," Grant told the jittery politicians in Washington, D.C.

In the worst of this holocaust, Grant never forgot he was fighting men who had been classmates and friends. When George Pickett's wife gave birth to a son, the men in Pickett's division celebrated the news with bonfires. Grant sent scouts to find out why the enemy was celebrating. When the scouts told him the reason, Grant turned to an aide. "Haven't we some kindling on this side of the lines? Why don't we strike a light for the young Pickett?"

Soon bonfires were glowing all along the Union lines. A few days later, under a flag of truce, Grant sent the Picketts a baby's silver service engraved:

"To George Pickett, Jr. From his father's friends, U.S. Grant, Rufus Ingalls, George Suckley."

In the West, William Tecumseh Sherman was marching to fame on Grant's order "to get into the interior of the enemy's country as far as you can, inflicting all the damage you can against their war resources." Advancing into Georgia, Sherman refused to attack the entrenched enemy. Instead, he maneuvered three army corps from flank to flank, swinging the outermost one as much as fifty miles to get behind the Confederate position and force them to retreat.

An awed rebel prisoner told one Union soldier: "Sherman ought to get on a high hill and command: 'Attention! Kingdoms by right wheel!'" Another captured rebel groaned. "Sherman'll never go to hell. He'll flank the devil and make Heaven in spite of the odds."

To back up his soldiers, Sherman used all the military skill West Point had to offer. Field telegraphers ran their wires right into the front lines so Sherman could communicate with the men under fire. Ahead of the army swarmed engineers who mapped the terrain and rushed their drawings back to "dark wagons"—darkrooms on wheels—where film could be developed. Here the drawings were photographed, and copies made for Sherman's staff and field commanders.

When the retreating Confederates burned bridges, Sherman's engineers replaced them in a matter of hours. They stretched canvas over already constructed frames, then planked them. Soon more than one Southern soldier was convinced that Sherman could do anything. When word arrived that Confederate cavalry had wrecked a railroad tunnel in the Union army's rear, a discouraged rebel said: "Sherman carries a duplicate."

Sherman's own men also became convinced that he knew almost everything. Once a private wandered past and found Sherman sleeping against a tree. "A pretty way we are commanded when our generals are lying drunk beside the road," the soldier growled.

"Stop, my man," shouted Sherman, leaping to his feet. "I'm not drunk. While you were sleeping last night I was planning for you, sir; now I was taking a nap."

The word went through the army. "Uncle Billy sleeps with one eye and one ear open."

Following Grant's example during the Vicksburg, Mississippi, campaign, Sherman abandoned his supply wagons. He figured to the last decimal point how much his men could carry on their backs. As he invaded Georgia, he had census reports of every country in the state to tell him exactly where his men could forage.

After capturing Atlanta, Georgia, Sherman took the most daring gamble of the war. Instead of fighting the Confederate army opposing him, he decided to ignore it and cut a burning swath across Georgia to the sea. Asking Grant's permission to take the gamble, Sherman wrote: "If the North can march an army right through the South, it is proof positive that the North can prevail,"

Grant gave his approval. With 60,000 men, Sherman proceeded to "march off the map," cutting himself loose from railroad and even telegraph communications with the rest of the world. In London, the British *Army and Navy Gazette* declared: "If Sherman has really left his army in the air and started off without a base to march from Atlanta,

Georgia, to [the sea], he has done one of the most brilliant or one of the most foolish things ever performed by a military leader."

So dazzled was the nation, reporters began to ask Grant if he was annoyed because Sherman was getting so much attention. Grant lit a cigar. "Jealousy between General Sherman and me is impossible," he said.

On December 15, a month to the day after Sherman disappeared, his advance guard wired Washington, D.C., from Savannah, Georgia: "We have met with perfect success thus far. Troops in fine spirits and General Sherman nearby." People rushed into country roads, embraced each other on city streets shouting: "He's made it. Sherman's at Savannah."

Another West Point friendship was important in Sherman's triumph. When he turned his army's face to the sea, Sherman left behind him a 40,000-man Confederate army. It was led by John Bell Hood of the class of 1853, a daring, aggressive soldier. Sherman knew Hood might march in the opposite direction, into Tennessee, hoping to win a victory there and shake the North's confidence.

But Sherman never so much as looked over his shoulder as he rumbled through the South's heartland to the sea. The Union commander in Tennessee was his classmate and closest friend, General George H. Thomas, the Virginian who had sacrificed so much to stay loyal to the Union. Sherman was sure "Old Tom" could handle Hood. "We recited together in the same section for four years, and served as lieutenants in the same regiment for ten years. Never since the world began did such absolute confidence exist between commander and commanded," Sherman said.

The only telegram Sherman sent before he left Atlanta was to George Thomas. He told him that if Hood invaded Tennessee, Sherman was was sure "you will whip him out of his boots."

Thomas was a soldier's soldier. He always insisted on thorough preparation for a battle. Critics accused him of being too cautious. But he got results by never deviating from one of the basic military ideas taught at West Point, concentration of force. All Thomas's preparations were aimed at delivering a blow against the enemy with overwhelming power.

At Mill Spring, Kentucky, in 1862, Thomas won the North's first clearcut victory over a Confederate army. He smashed 4,000 rebels into a fleeing rabble who abandoned their colors and their wounded. Thomas's 14th Army Corps soon became a bulwark in the series of battles for control of Tennessee and Kentucky. Somehow he communicated his rocklike character to his men. They became famous for their fierce defensive fighting.

In the fall of 1863, on the Tennessee battlefield named for a little creek called Chickamauga, the Union commander, William Rosecrans, West Point, 1842, lost both his nerve and his wits. He issued orders that caused his right wing and his center to collapse. Rosecrans then abandoned the battlefield, leaving Thomas in charge of the left wing, the only part of the army still a fighting force.

Grouping shattered regiments around his own unbroken lines, Thomas stood off the combined assault of Braxton Bragg's entire Confederate army. Here is how one of Thomas's soldiers described it years later: "Disaster is closing in everywhere. Yet under the shadow of a spreading oak is a grizzled soldier, calm, silent, immoveable, who resolves to hold the field until night comes." Thomas's stand on that September afternoon saved the Union army in the West. Reporters nicknamed him "the Rock of Chickamauga."

While Sherman marched toward the sea, Thomas waited in Nashville for John Bell Hood. Just as he and Sherman had suspected, Hood took his 40,000 men into Tennessee, hoping to regain control of that crucial state. His timing was good. Grant and Lee were still grappling in Virginia. The casualty lists of that awful struggle—in a single month Grant lost 60,000 men—had sent a shudder through the North. Hood's appearance before Nashville turned horror to panic.

The politicians in Washington, D.C., telegraphed orders to attack Hood immediately. Thomas ignored them. He let Hood sit on the hills outside Nashville while he prepared his battle plan and called in regiments on garrison duty, building his army to maximum strength. Finally, with an advantage of almost two to one over the depleted Confederates, on December 15, 1864, Thomas attacked. In two days of sledge hammer blows, he broke Hood's army into fragments. It was the end of the Confederacy in the West.

16

The Final Days

The Southern cause was in its death throes. The bravest and the best began to fall. Jeb Stuart rode out with worn horses and thinned ranks to meet a massive Federal cavalry raid led by Sheridan and Custer. They destroyed tons of vital supplies and equipment and threatened to overrun Richmond itself. A fierce fight boiled around Yellow Tavern, an abandoned inn about six miles from the southern capital.

Custer, noticing a Confederate battery in an exposed position on Stuart's flank, charged and captured it, rolling up that side of the Confederate line, forcing a disordered retreat. In the confusion, a Union cavalryman was able to ride close enough to Stuart to shoot him with a pistol. He died the next day.

When Robert E. Lee heard the news, he wept. No doubt he remembered the laughing cadet who visited him on Saturday afternoons at West Point. Weeks later, Lee told a friend he could "scarcely think of him without weeping."

Powell Hill, now a major general, rode to rally his famed "Light Division" during another Grant attack. In the woods, he and an escorting sergeant encountered Union skirmishers. Hill tried the trick Stuart had used at Bull Run. "Our men are here. Surrender your arms," he shouted, riding toward them, pistol in hand. But the Yankees were veterans now, no longer easily fooled. They killed Hill with a bullet in the heart.

Only emotion held the battered Confederate army together now. At its center was a devotion to Robert E. Lee. Twice in the struggle with Grant, Lee rode to the front to rally his men and to lead them in a counterattack. Both times, the men refused to advance. "General Lee to the rear," they roared. Aides finally seized the bridle of Lee's horse and led him to safety. Then the gaunt men in gray flung themselves forward again to blunt the Union assault.

When Grant was besieging the intricate fortifications of Petersburg, outside Richmond, Lee often rode out to the forward outposts to study the Union positions. One morning late in November 1864, he climbed onto a platform inside one of the trenches, exposing most of his body to Northern sharpshooters. Immediately, Brigadier General Achibald Gracie stepped in front of him. He was the New York cadet whose gallantry had won Lee's admiration when he was superintendent. Quietly, Gracie began pointing out various northern units to Lee.

"General Gracie," Lee said. "You should not expose yourself so much."

"If I should not, General Lee, why should you, the commander in chief?" Gracie replied.

Only then did Lee realize that Gracie was deliberately standing between him and the Union rifles. With a small nod, Lee climbed down from the platform and continued along the bottom of the trench. A few days later, a Union sniper killed Gracie.

Around the same time, Grant too experienced the pain of a personal loss. Sherman reported from

Atlanta that one of the best of the Grant men, General James Birdseye McPherson, had been killed by a bullet in the heart while riding to rally his men against a Confederate assault. "The country has lost one of its best soldiers—and I have lost my best friend," Grant said. He retreated to his tent and remained there for hours, alone with his grief.

To civilians, the war seemed to have its own evil life. People wondered if the bloodshed would last another twenty years. They did not realize that Grant's relentless assaults, his tireless attempts to turn the flank of the Confederate army and get into its rear, were forcing Lee to stretch his dwindling brigades farther and farther apart. As 1865 dawned, Lee was holding more than forty miles of trenches and forts with less than 1,000 men to a mile.

In March 1865, a series of terrific assaults tore the Confederate defenses apart. Lee was forced to abandon Richmond and retreat south. Grant's pursuit was, in the word's of one military historian, "one of the best operations of its type in the history of warfare." While one part of his army smashed at Lee's rear guard, Sheridan raced ahead with another huge force to block the escape routes. When Lee's half-starved, exhausted men stumbled into the little village of Appomattox Court House, they found rank after rank of Sheridan's blue-clad troopers on the road ahead of them.

Lee told a courier from Jefferson Davis that the war was ending "just I have expected it would end from the first." With a sigh, he summoned his officers and asked their advice. What would the country think if he surrendered? One man replied: "There is no country. There has been no country for a year or more. You are the country to these men."

Lee turned to his second in command, huge, bearded Pete Longstreet, and asked his opinion.

"Will the sacrifice of the army help the cause in other quarters?" Longstreet asked.

"I think not," Lee said.

"Then your situation speaks for itself," Longstreet said.

Edward Porter Alexander of West Point's class of 1857 was Lee's commander of artillery. Speaking for the younger officers, he asked Lee to disband the army, order the men to "scatter like rabbits and partridges in the bushes," and fight on as guerrillas.

Lee recoiled. He saw that a guerrilla war would create hatred between the North and the South that might take centuries to heal. "The men would have no rations, be under no discipline. They'd have to rob and plunder," he said.

Alexander flushed. Later he said that he felt Lee was speaking from a moral plane so far above him, he was ashamed even to have made the suggestion. But he could not resist arguing back. "A little more blood or less now makes no difference. Spare the men who have fought under you for four years the mortification of having to ask Grant for terms and have him say unconditional surrender. General, spare us the mortification of having you get that reply."

"General Grant will not demand unconditional surrender," Lee replied. "He will give us as honorable terms as we have a right to ask or expect."

Amazing statement! Here was a general on the edge of total disaster, expecting the enemy commander he had frustrated for twelve terrible months to give him honorable terms. What else but the spirit of West Point, the brotherhood of the corps, could have given Lee such confidence?

Sheridan was massing his troopers for a final assault. He rode along the blue ranks, growling: "Now smash 'em, I tell you smash 'em." Just as his bugles blew the charge, a Confederate officer rode through the lines with a letter from Robert E. Lee to Ulysses S. Grant. General Lee asked for a meeting to discuss the surrender of his army.

17

Brotherhood Restored

When Grant heard that Lee had offered to surrender, he displayed, in the words of a newspaper-man with him at the time "no excultaltion ... no sign of joy. Instead of flushing from excitement, he clenched his teeth, compressed his lips and became very pale."

Rather than keep Lee waiting, Grant rode to the surrender site in his mud-spattered field uniform. "What General Lee's feelings were, I do not know," he later wrote. "But my own feelings were sad and depressed."

Here Grant was displaying his instinctive sympathy for the gallant losers. His staff felt the same way. When Grant ordered Lee's note read aloud to them, someone proposed three cheers. Most of them burst into tears instead.

Grant and Lee met in the parlor of a white-pillared house owned by Major Wilmer McClean. By odd coincidence, McClean had owned the farm at Bull Run where the first battle of the war had taken place. Grant was embarrassed to find Lee had dressed in his best uniform. The Union commander apologized for his tattered appearance and asked Lee if he remembered a night long ago, when they had met in Mexico. "I have always remembered your appearance," Grant said. "I think I should have recognized you anywhere."

Lee replied that he recalled the meeting, but admitted he had been unable to remember "a single feature" of Grant's face.

Still trying to ease the tension and pain of the meeting, Grant chatted for several minutes about Mexican War days. Finally Lee asked him if he was ready to discuss surrender terms.

Grant stated them promptly and concisely. "The officers and men surrendered to be paroled and disqualified from taking up arms again until properly exchanged, and all arms, ammunition and supplies to be delivered up as captured Property."

Lee nodded. "Those are about the terms I expected." At his suggestion, Grant sat down at a table and wrote them out. Only then did Lee realize that the agreement would not permit the southern cavalrymen and artillerymen to keep their horses, many of which they owned.

Grant pondered for a moment. "I will not change the terms as they are written," he finally said. "But I will instruct the officers to let all the men who claim to own a horse or a mule take the animals home with them to work their little farms."

"This will have the best possible effect upon my men," Lee said. "It will be very gratifying and it will do much toward conciliating our people."

The two generals then discussed the problem of feeding Lee's men. Grant turned to his commissary general, the man in charge of the Union army's supplies. "General Lee has about a thousand or fifteen hundred of our people prisoners and they are faring the same as his men, but he tells me his haven't anything. Can you send them some rations?"

Within the hour, three days' rations—fresh beef, salt, bread, coffee, and sugar—were flowing into the Confederate lines. They were soon followed by Federal troops who, with Grant's permission, shared the food they carried in their knapsacks with the starving southerners.

When the news of the surrender reached the Union army, bands began playing and some artillerymen fired victory salutes. Grant ordered an instant stop to such celebrations. "The Rebels are our countrymen again," he said. Later that night, when someone told Grant that he should have held Lee and his generals for trial as traitors, the Union commander said: "I'll keep the terms no matter who's opposed."

Even before the surrender was signed, George Armstrong Custer called to one of his 1860 classmates, "Let's go see if we can find Cowan." They rode to the edge of a stream separating the two armies and asked a southern officer to find Robert V. Cowan of North Carolina, who had been two classes behind Custer.

A few minutes later, Cowan rode his horse across the shallow stream. "Hello you damned red-headed rebel," Custer said, pounding him on the back.

While the three West Pointers were talking, General Lee rode by on his way to see Grant. Lee sternly ordered Cowan to return to the Confederate side of the stream. Custer, true to form, signalled the moment Lee was out of sight, and Cowan returned to exchange more West Point news.

The moment the surrender became official, Custer rode to the Confederate camp in search of more friends. He found Gimlet Lea and invited him to dinner. Then he was face to face with another rambunctious cavalryman, Fitzhugh Lee. With a whoop, these two birds of a feather embraced each other and rolled on the ground, laughing like schoolboys.

In Richmond, not long after the city was occupied by Federal troops, George Pickett's wife answered a knock on her door, carrying her baby son on her arm. There stood "a tall gaunt, sad-faced man in ill-fitting clothes" who asked in a Kentucky accent if this was George Pickett's home. When the young wife said it was, the stranger said: "I'm Abraham Lincoln."

"The President!" gasped Mrs. Pickett.

Lincoln shook his head. "No, ma'am, no, ma'am. Just Abraham Lincoln, George's old friend."

Lincoln took the baby in his arms and gave the boy a kiss. He handed him back to his mother and said: "Tell your father, the rascal, that I forgive him for the sake of that kiss and those bright eyes."

Jefferson Davis, embittered by his four-year ordeal, refused to admit the war was lost. He rode south to rally the only southern army left, a remnant that was trying to block the onward march of Sherman's host. The army's commander, Joseph Johnston, told Davis further resistance would only waste lives. Riding farther south, Davis was captured by Union cavalry under the command of one of the "Grant men," James Wilson.

At Greensboro, North Carolina, William Tecumseh Sherman accepted the surrender of Joseph Johnston's army. Sherman's terms were even more generous than Grant's at Appomattox. He let Johnston sign his name first on the surrender document. He issued ten days rations to all the captured soldiers and loaned them "enough farm animals to insure a crop."

Sherman ordered his men to encourage the southern civilians in their vicinity to go back to their jobs. His goal was "to restore the relations of friendship among our fellow citizens and countrymen." General Johnston, a man not given to emotional statements, wrote to Sherman, "The enlarged patriotism exhibited in your orders reconciles me to what I have previously regarded as the misfortune of my life, that of having you to encounter in the field."

None were more eager than West Pointers to follow Abraham Lincoln down the path of reconciliation that the president had outlined in his second inaugural address. They were already trying to bind up the nation's wounds, to care for those who had borne the battle and their widows and their orphans. Such conduct seemed natural, almost logical, for men who still believed, in spite of four years of war, in the brotherhood of the corps.

18

Peacemakers

The dream of swift reconciliation between the North and South vanished when a fanatic blasted a bullet through Abraham Lincoln's brain a week after Appomattox. The United States reeled into decades of antagonism between the two sections. But West Pointers kept trying to achieve a reunion of minds and hearts.

Ohioan Morris Schaff told of riding a night train from Montgomery to Atlanta a few months after the end of the war. It stopped at a lonely station in Alabama and Charles B. Ball, the handsome former first sergeant of Company A, entered the car. He had fought as a cavalryman in the war, rising to the rank of colonel.

"As soon as he rocognized me," Schaff said, "he quickened his step and met me with such unaffected cordiality that the car seemed to glow with new lamps. I would not have been hurt had he merely bowed and passed on. I realized how much there had been to embitter. Yet he sat and we talked over old times half the night. I could not help wondering as he parted from me whether I could have shown so much magnanimity had the South conquered the North and had I come home in rags, to find the old farm desolate. I doubt it."

In the War Department in Washington, D.C., General Grant greeted his old friend Pete Longstreet with a smile and a handshake. He locked arms with the man who had been Robert E. Lee's second in command and said: "Pete, let's go back to the good old times and play a game of brag [a favorite army card game] as we used to."

That evening, Grant entertained Longstreet at his home and invited numerous friends from their West Point days to the reunion. As Longstreet left, Grant asked if he wanted to have a pardon. Congress had passed a law requiring Confederate officers to ask for a pardon for their rebellion against the Union. Without a pardon, a man could not vote or hold public office.

Longstreet told Grant he did not feel he had done anything that required a pardon. Grant told him he would persuade the new president, Andrew Johnson, to give Longstreet amnesty. The next day, Grant gave "Old Pete" a letter to give to the president, urging Johnson to include Longstreet on his amnesty list. The president read the letter and shook his head. "There are three persons of the South who can never receive amnesty," he said. "Mr. Davis, General Lee and yourself. You have given the Union cause too much trouble."

Grant took matters into his own hands. If Longstreet was too stubborn to ask for a pardon, Grant would do it for him. When a list of officers from Georgia requesting pardons arrived at the War Department, Grant put Pete's name on it without consulting him. Longstreet got the pardon and prospered as a businessman in New Orleans. But he got into trouble when he wrote a letter to a newspaper, urging Louisiana to give Negroes the right to vote. Angry southerners boycotted his business.

Once more, Ulysses Grant came to Old Pete's rescue. In 1868, Grant was elected president. One of his first appointments was Longstreet as surveyor of customs at New Orleans.

The spirit of Appomattox had inspired the poet Walt Whitman to exclaim: "Affection shall solve the problems of freedom yet." West Pointers kept trying to use this affection to heal the wounds of war. In 1869, northerners formed an Association of Graduates. Major General Robert Anderson, defender of Fort Sumter, wrote a letter to graduates north and south, urging them to attend the first meeting, which took place on May 22, 1869.

For the first few meetings, no southerners appeared. Finally, Charles Davies of the class of 1815, who had been too old to fight in the war, persuaded Francis H. Smith of the class of 1833, the founder of the Virginia Military Institute, to stay at his house near West Point as his guest. Smith accepted and was deeply moved by the warmth of the reception he received from northerners at the reunion. He went back to Virginia and urged other southern graduates to attend the meetings. Their numbers grew rapidly.

When West Point's centennial was celebrated in 1902, among the chief speakers was Edward Porter Alexander of the class of 1857. He had been Robert E. Lee's chief of artillery, the young firebrand who recommended that the Confederates fight on as guerrillas. Alexander and James Longstreet headed a veritable column of southern veterans who came to the celebration. When Alexander mentioned Old Pete by name, the audience burst into cheers.

Looking back at the war, Alexander declared "it was best for the South that the cause was lost." He said that if the right to secede was now offered to the South as a gift, "we would reject it as a proposition of suicide."

Alexander recalled to his listeners those six wonderful days after Appomattox, before Lincoln's assassination, when it seemed possible that the nation would be reunited without bitterness. He spoke of "the friendliness, courtesy, generosity" that Grant's army displayed.

Now, Alexander said, the wounds of war were finally healed. Only one question remained. "Was all the agony endured for the lost cause but as water spilled upon sand? Was all our blood shed in vain?"

"No," Alexander said. "A thousand times no. We have given to our children a proud memory and to history new names, to be a theme and an inspiration for unborn generations. The heroes of future wars will emulate our Lees and Jacksons."

The southern West Pointers did not join a lost cause. They were born into it, Alexander said. "We fought it out to its remotest end and suffered to the very utmost its dying aches and pains. They have proven to be the birth pangs of a new nation, in whose career we are proud to own and to bear a part."

Finally, Alexander offered a tribute to West Point, "who taught us not the skill to unravel conflicting political creeds but rather to illustrate by our lives manly courage and loyalty to convictions."

With a roar, the old men who had been young in 1861 struggled to their feet. The band struck up "The Star-Spangled Banner," the same song it had played on a night long ago at a divided West Point. The gray-haired veterans threw their arms around each other and wept.

The next day, Secretary of War Elihu Root said what was obvious to everyone. "No army inspired by the spirit of the military academy can ever endanger a country's liberty or desert its country's flag."

Bibliography

Catton, Bruce. *Grant Takes Command*. Boston: Little, Brown, 1969.

Davis, Burke. *Sherman's March*. New York: Random House, 1980.

Eaton, Clement. *Jefferson Davis*. New York: The Free Press, 1977.

Freeman, Douglas Southall. *R. E. Lee*. New York: Charles Scribner's Sons, 1936.

Hassler, Warren W. *General George B. McClellan, Shield of the Union*. Baton Rouge: Louisiana State University Press, 1957.

Hutton, Paul A. *Phil Sheridan and his Army*. Lincoln: University of Nebraska Press, 1985.

Lewis, Lloyd. *Captain Sam Grant*. Boston: Little Brown, 1950.

————. *Sherman, Fighting Prophet*. Boston: Harcourt, Brace, 1932.

McCartney, Clarence Edward Noble. *Grant and his Generals*. New York: McBride Co., 1953.

Pemberton, John C. *Pemberton*. Chapel Hill: University of North Carolina Press, 1942.

Robertson, James I. *A. P. Hill, the Story of a Confederate Warrior*. New York: Random House, 1987.

Tucker, Glenn. *Hancock The Superb*. Indianapolis: Bobbs Merrill, 1960.

Urwin, Gregory *J. Custer Victorious: The Civil War Battles of George Armstrong Custer*. Madison, N.J.: Fairleigh Dickinson University Press, 1982.

Vandiver, Frank. *Mighty Stonewall*. Westport, Conn.: Greenwood Press, 1974.

About the Author

Thomas Fleming has written a dozen distinguished history books, including biographies of George Washington, Thomas Jefferson and Benjamin Franklin. He is equally well known for his historical novels, such as *Liberty Tavern* and *The Spoils of War*. His history of West Point, published in 1969, was hailed by the *New York Times* as "the best book ever written about the U.S. Military Academy." He lives in New York with his wife, Alice, who is a prolific writer of books for young readers.